The
Literacy Coach's
COMPANION
PreK–3

For those who coach us in literacy and in life:

*To Pat "Lucy" Chapman, a dear friend and former colleague,
who has supported my professional journey every step of the way.*
Maryann

*To my family, who daily remind me of the
enduring joys of fatherhood, and especially for Kate,
who lets me know every day that love is a many-splendored thing.*
Bob

*To my wife, Hattie, and my baby boys,
Charles and Benjamin, who are my teachers in life.*
Brian

The
Literacy Coach's
COMPANION
PreK–3

Maryann Mraz
Bob Algozzine
Brian Kissel

Foreword by Nancy D. Padak

A Joint Publication

CORWIN
PRESS
A SAGE Company

INTERNATIONAL
Reading
Association

For information:

Corwin Press
A SAGE Company
2455 Teller Road
Thousand Oaks, California 91320
www.corwinpress.com

SAGE Ltd.
1 Oliver's Yard
55 City Road
London EC1Y 1SP
United Kingdom

SAGE India Pvt. Ltd.
B 1/I 1 Mohan Cooperative
   Industrial Area
Mathura Road, New Delhi 110 044
India

SAGE Asia-Pacific Pte. Ltd.
33 Pekin Street #02-01
Far East Square
Singapore 048763

International Reading Association
800 Barksdale Road
PO Box 8139
Newark, DE 19714-8139
www.reading.org

Printed in the United States of America.

Library of Congress Cataloging-in-Publication Data

Mraz, Maryann.
  The literacy coach's companion, prek-3 / Maryann Mraz, Bob Algozzine, Brian Kissel.
     p. cm.
  "A Joint Publication with the International Reading Association."
  Includes bibliographical references and index.
  ISBN 978-1-4129-6072-4 (cloth)
  ISBN 978-1-4129-6073-1 (pbk.)
  IRA Stock Number: 9199

  1. Education, Preschool. 2. Literacy—Study and teaching. I. Algozzine, Robert.
II. Kissel, Brian. III. Title.

LB1140.2.M73 2009   2008026479
372.21—dc22

This book is printed on acid-free paper.

08   09   10   11   12   10 9 8 7 6 5 4 3 2 1

Acquisitions Editor:	Carol Chambers Collins
Editorial Assistant:	Brett Ory
Production Editor:	Libby Larson
Copy Editor:	Jennifer Withers
Typesetter:	C&M Digitals (P) Ltd.
Proofreader:	Gail Fay
Indexer:	Maria Sosnowski
Cover Designer:	Scott Van Atta

Contents

Foreword

Until about a decade ago, thinking about coaches usually brought sports to our minds, maybe Vince Lombardi or Phil Jackson. Now educational coaches have joined their athletic colleagues. In some ways, the roles of these two types of coaches are similar. Consider these quotes from Vince Lombardi, legendary coach of the Green Bay Packers, for example, but think about them from the perspective of a literacy coach:

- "Coaches who can outline plays on the blackboard are a dime a dozen. The ones who win get inside their player and motivate."
- "The dictionary is the only place that 'success' comes before 'work.' Hard work is the price we must pay for success."

Of course, there are differences between literacy coaches and athletic coaches too. In this book, *The Literacy Coach's Companion, PreK–3,* Maryann Mraz, Bob Algozzine, and Brian Kissel provide a wealth of advice for literacy coaches who work with teachers of young children.

As anyone who has taught students of different ages knows, some aspects of the effective teaching of reading apply to all students, yet other aspects are affected by students' ages and developmental needs. So it is with literacy coaching at various levels. Some characteristics of effective literacy coaches are applicable to any level of schooling, but primary teachers may well have different needs than high school teachers. One of the major strengths of this book is its focus—coaching in early and elementary literacy programs (prekindergarten–Grade 3). The authors believe that preK–Grade 3 teachers have unique needs; they have provided suggestions to support coaches as they seek to build strong literacy communities within classrooms and schools for young children.

So much helpful information is packed into this slim volume. The authors have blended research, theory, and practice into readable chapters about topics critical to effective coaching: roles and responsibilities, the whys and hows of conferring with teachers, ways to use data to establish instructional priorities, how to foster the development of collaborative teams, and models for professional development. Chapters can be read in any order, which adds to the usefulness of the book. Readers can begin with chapters that address their current needs and dip into the book again when their needs change.

Literacy coaches are very busy professionals. Many maintain part-time teaching schedules in addition to their coaching responsibilities. For this reason, they need resources that are research-based, practical, and readable—even in the few minutes they may have between tasks. The format of the book adds to its utility. Each chapter begins with a bulleted list of topics and ends with questions designed to promote additional reflection. Key points frequently appear in bulleted lists throughout the chapters as well. Moreover, the authors provide lots of authentic coaching artifacts that can be used as is or adapted to suit a particular coaching context, such as daily, weekly, and yearly schedules for coaches; teacher-coach conference forms; and classroom observation protocols. These resources will be particularly helpful for new coaches, although experienced coaches will also want to peruse them for revision ideas.

Another feature of the book—the "Voices From the Field" component—adds to both the usefulness and the readability of the volume. These vignettes from literacy coaches provide insights, examples, and advice. Experienced coaches tell about the triumphs and challenges of their job while explaining the qualities they know to be important to successful coaching. Their stories and their advice are sure to be of interest to both present and future literacy coaches.

> *"Good teams become great ones when members trust each other enough to surrender the Me for the We."*
>
> —Phil Jackson

Phil Jackson is reflecting on his experiences as an NBA coach, but he could just as well be describing a literacy coach's stance in a school-wide literacy improvement effort. Mraz, Algozzine, and Kissel have provided a practical, research-based guide for literacy coaches who want to help good teachers and schools become great ones.

—Nancy D. Padak
Distinguished Professor, Education
Kent State University

Acknowledgments

Many people have contributed wisdom and guidance to our professional growth and to our work on this project. Collectively, we are grateful to our colleagues who contributed greatly to writing this book, including Rebecca Kavel for her suggestions about the organizational aspects of literacy coaching and Kate Algozzine and Tina McClanahan for helping us to broaden our vision of the literacy coach's role. We are also thankful for the interest and support of Carol Collins and the outstanding team of professionals at Corwin Press and the International Reading Association with whom we worked in producing the book. The feedback from our reviewers was instrumental in helping us to shape the form and content of this book. We thank them for their thoughtful comments and suggestions.

Maryann Mraz is thankful for the opportunity to work with an exceptional team of literacy coaches and literacy leaders in Charlotte-Mecklenburg Schools, including Julie Babb, Kimberly Foxworth, and Jackie Moore. Bob Algozzine is grateful for what he learned from Maryann and Brian while writing this book. Brian Kissel is thankful to Jan Wood and Bronwyn McLemore, who worked with him as a prekindergarten literacy coach in Duval County, Florida, and to Kathy Smith, who was his elementary school coaching partner at West Riverside Elementary School in Jacksonville, Florida. All three were instrumental in shaping his notions of coaching and working with adult learners.

Publisher's Acknowledgments

Corwin Press gratefully acknowledges the contributions of the following people:

Tracy Carbone, Reading Recovery Teacher
Rocky River Elementary, Monroe, North Carolina

Marcella (Marcy) Emberger, Education Consultant
New Brunswick, Canada

Sharon D. Kruse, Professor
University of Akron, Akron, Ohio

Connie Molony, Reading Intervention Specialist
Fargo Public Schools, Fargo, North Dakota

Dale E. Moxley, Principal
Round Lake Elementary, Lake County, Florida

Susan B. Neuman, Professor, Educational Studies
University of Michigan, Ann Arbor, Michigan

Rosemarye T. Taylor, Associate Professor
    of Educational Leadership
University of Central Florida, Orlando, Florida

About the Authors

Maryann Mraz is an Associate Professor in the Reading and Elementary Education Department in the College of Education at the University of North Carolina at Charlotte. She teaches graduate courses in literacy education as well as literacy methods courses, and she frequently provides professional development workshops to teachers and literacy coaches. She is the author of numerous books, chapters, and articles on literacy education, including *Evidenced-Based Instruction in Reading: A Professional Development Guide to Phonemic Awareness* (2008) with Nancy Padak and Timothy Rasinski and *Teaching Literacy in Sixth Grade* (2005) with Karen Wood. She earned her PhD from Kent State University. Her professional interests include literacy coaching, professional development, early literacy, and content area literacy.

Bob Algozzine is a Professor in the Department of Educational Leadership in the College of Education at the University of North Carolina at Charlotte. He has been a special education classroom teacher and college professor for more than 30 years in public schools and universities in New York, Virginia, Pennsylvania, Florida, and North Carolina. He is currently the Director of the Behavior and Reading Improvement Center at the University of North Carolina at Charlotte. Textbooks he has written are used in teacher preparation courses around the country. He has been a featured speaker at local, state, national, and international professional conferences and is widely recognized as an expert on effective teaching and special education.

 **Brian Kissel** is an Assistant Professor in the Department of Reading and Elementary Education in the College of Education at the University of North Carolina at Charlotte. He teaches both graduate and undergraduate courses in writing development and language arts. Previously, he worked as an elementary school teacher, an elementary-based literacy coach, and a prekindergarten literacy coach. He continues to work with literacy coaches in the Charlotte area. He earned his PhD from the University of Virginia. His current research interests include literacy coaching and writing acquisition in prekindergarten children.

About the Contributors

Stephen Hancock is an Assistant Professor in the Department of Reading and Elementary Education in the College of Education at the University of North Carolina at Charlotte. He served as a teacher's assistant, preschool teacher, and elementary school teacher in Grades K–3 for 15 years. He earned his PhD from the Ohio State University. His research interests include diversity awareness, urban education, and minority achievement.

Paola Pilonieta is an Assistant Professor in the Department of Reading and Elementary Education in the College of Education at the University of North Carolina at Charlotte. She taught first grade for five years and earned her PhD in reading from the University of Miami. Her research interests include comprehension instruction in the primary grades and teacher education.

Introduction

In recent years, literacy coaches have become a more visible part of the school's literacy team. A number of issues have emerged as this new literacy coaching role has unfolded and as the role of the coach has shifted from that of a reading specialist who works directly with students who struggle to learn, to a coach who works with teachers to improve instructional practices. Those issues include defining an effective and consistent role for the literacy coach; training coaches to interact collaboratively with teachers to establish productive learning communities; communicating the changing role of the coach to school leaders; helping coaches to develop critical content knowledge that can be used to support the work of teachers and, in turn, the literacy learning of students; and supporting coaches as they seek to develop their own content knowledge and coaching skills.

This guidebook is intended to be one resource for addressing these issues. During the course of our careers in the field of education, we have worked as teachers, literacy coaches, and administrators. Currently, in our work as university professors, we work collaboratively with literacy coaches who strive to address the diverse literacy needs of their school communities while navigating their multifaceted, and often ambiguous, roles as coaches.

In this book, we focus on coaching in early and elementary literacy programs (prekindergarten through Grade 3) to address the unique needs of these programs and to provide suggestions that will support coaches as they seek to build strong literacy communities within their schools. It is our hope that our combination of research-based content information, practical guidelines, authentic examples, and organizational templates will provide literacy coaches with a meaningful and useful framework for embarking on their work with teachers.

Throughout the chapters, we provide coaches with suggestions and examples, drawn from real classrooms, that can be used and adapted to meet the needs of their own school communities. Those examples include daily, weekly, and yearly schedules; letters to teachers; teacher-coach conference forms; classroom observation protocols; sample dialogues between teachers and coaches; and sample responses of coaches to challenging assessment and behavioral issues of students.

Each chapter includes a "Voices From the Field" component: accounts from real literacy coaches who provide both insight into the coaching experience and advice to those pursuing this important role. These coaches explain the triumphs and challenges of their job. Along the way, they offer their views on their role as literacy coaches, the qualities they feel are important to successful coaching, examples of what they have learned from their experiences, and advice for present and future literacy coaches. At the end of each chapter, discussion questions and continuous learning suggestions are provided in the "Next Steps: Professional Development Suggestions" section. These ideas are intended to help readers reflect on and apply the information contained in each of the chapters as they pursue their own professional growth as literacy coaches.

In Chapter 1, "Your Role and the Task at Hand: The Responsibilities of a Coach in Supporting Effective Literacy Instruction," we discuss recent changes in the role of the literacy coach, as well as recommendations for that role. This chapter also provides examples of effective teaching principles (i.e., planning, managing, delivering, and evaluating classroom instruction) with relevance for coaching in early and elementary literacy classrooms.

In Chapter 2, "The Nuts and Bolts: Scheduling, Organizing, and Documenting," we address the basic organizational issues that are so important for establishing a framework through which effective coaching can occur. Here, we deal with issues such as establishing an office, planning a schedule, and organizing training materials for teachers and teacher assistants. Also included in this chapter are sample schedules and organizational templates, and a variety of formats for documenting observations and conferences.

In Chapter 3, "The Heart of the Matter: Conferring With Teachers," we offer recommendations to the literacy coach for establishing effective communication with teachers. We provide vignettes highlighting common situations that can be particularly challenging for literacy coaches, such as establishing collaborative relationships with reluctant teachers, identifying areas in individual classrooms that would benefit from change, prioritizing and communicating needed changes with teachers, and approaching teachers who do not perceive a need for change. We discuss how a coach can guide teachers in the use of genuine inquiry that encourages them to reflect on and improve their teaching practices.

In Chapter 4, "Assessment: Using Data to Inform Literacy Instruction," we provide foundations and practical illustrations for coaches to use when helping teachers to use assessment to inform instruction in early literacy programs. We focus on practical activities, including how to select and implement appropriate assessments, how to interpret results, and how to use outcomes to inform classroom teaching practices. Vignettes provide examples of some common literacy concerns that often emerge from student assessment data, along with responses that a literacy coach might provide to a teacher to address those concerns. We identify critical aspects of classroom-based assessments and decision making, explore elements of curriculum-based and functional assessments, and focus on how to use progress monitoring to improve the fit between testing and teaching.

In Chapter 5, "Learning Communities: Supporting Collaborative Teamwork," we establish and discuss the importance of developing trust, establishing unified missions, organizing and managing small- and large-group meetings and learning opportunities, and celebrating successes. Bringing about change in early literacy environments is more effective when professionals work together as teams that are well organized and committed to successful and sustainable teaching and learning outcomes. In this chapter, we illustrate how to create and support growth-oriented professional learning communities by helping teachers set attainable goals, establish appropriate priorities, share knowledge and skills, learn from supportive and corrective feedback, build trusting relationships, and work with administrators to define the coach's role within the school.

In Chapter 6, "Ongoing Growth: Supporting Professional Development," we extend beyond the coach-teacher relationship to consider professional development from a schoolwide perspective. Here, we discuss the characteristics of high-quality professional development initiatives, strategies to support change, and guidelines for working with school administrators to implement professional development initiatives that support ongoing professional growth for both literacy coaches and teachers.

The appendix, "For Further Reading: An Annotated Bibliography of Resources on Literacy Instruction and Coaching," concludes the book with resources for content-related professional development initiatives directed by coaches, and an annotated list of books, articles, and Web resources that pertain to developing and implementing a successful early literacy program. Clearly, the topics of content and coaching in early literacy (preK–3) classrooms are far more than a single book can cover. We hope that the resources provided in this appendix will serve as a starting point for the continued learning on topics of both content and coaching.

1

Your Role and the Task at Hand

The Responsibilities of a Coach in Supporting Effective Literacy Instruction

In this chapter, we

- discuss recent changes in the role of the literacy coach
- identify and discuss current recommendation for roles of the literacy coach
- identify the qualities that make coaches effective
- provide examples of effective teaching activities with relevance for coaching early literacy

The importance of effective early literacy instruction is widely accepted: patterns of school failure that begin in the early school years persist as children move into the elementary grades (Strickland, 2002). The achievement gap between high-socioeconomic and low-socioeconomic students has long been a source of concern for educators and policy makers. The passage of the No Child Left Behind Act of 2001 (U.S. Department of Education, 2002), including the Reading First and Early Reading First programs, has intensified the attention focused on accountability and achievement in early literacy education (Mraz & Kissel, 2007). Having literacy coaches in schools who are prepared to address children's learning needs by providing guidance for classroom teachers has been recognized as a necessary component for improving the quality of literacy education in schools for some time (International Reading Association [IRA], 2004). However, ideas about the nature of that role and the direction it should take have evolved in recent years.

How Has the Role of the Literacy Coach Changed?

Before the title *literacy coach* was commonly used, reading specialists were hired in schools to work directly with struggling readers in small groups or pullout programs where students typically received intense, skill-based instruction outside of the regular classroom (Pipes, 2004). Often, there was little collaboration between the classroom teacher and the reading specialist about the type of instruction each student received, and concerns were frequently voiced about the effectiveness of the pullout program model (Allington & Walmsley, 2007; Dole, 2004).

VOICES FROM THE FIELD

"I learned that I really had to define what it is that I did on a daily basis. I came up with an acronym to remind myself of my job responsibilities. The acronym is COACH. C is for building community because it is so important to build relationships with the teachers I work with. O is for observing. I think one of the biggest parts of my job is to go into classrooms and just watch and learn. A is for analyzing. Once I observe, it is so important for me to help teachers analyze what they did as instructors. C is for communicating. It is vital that the teacher and I talk about what happened in the classroom and keep an open line of communication. H is for help. I am there to help the teacher realize her best potential. I'm not there to evaluate or talk down to the teacher. I am there to help her—to build her up."

Elizabeth

In response to concerns over the low reading achievement of many students as reflected in standardized test scores, educators and policy makers sought ways to improve reading proficiency levels. The options for providing reading education support expanded, and the role of the reading specialist was more broadly defined. Communication and collaboration between reading specialist and teachers were increasingly emphasized. Ongoing professional development initiatives designed to increase the knowledge and skills of all educators were more commonly implemented (Bean, Trovato, & Hamilton, 1995; Moxley & Taylor, 2006; Mraz, Vacca, & Vintinner, 2008).

As these changes occurred, the benefits of having literacy professionals in schools became increasingly apparent: literacy professionals could support teachers in improving instructional practices to enhance school reading programs and, in turn, increase student achievement in reading (Lapp, Fisher, Flood, & Frey, 2003; Shaw, Smith, Chesler, & Romeo, 2005). Literacy coaching began to find wide acceptance in professional circles as one way of addressing the literacy needs of schools, teachers, and students.

Changing expectations for the role of literacy coaches produced new titles and new job descriptions. Titles used to describe literacy coaches include the following:

- learning specialist
- literacy facilitator
- language arts specialist
- language arts coach
- curriculum specialist
- instructional specialist
- instructional coach
- academic facilitator

The jobs literacy coaches fulfill in schools can be as varied as their titles. Some focus specifically on supporting classroom teachers in their daily implementation of the school's literacy program (IRA, 2006). Others support teachers by working across subject areas or by providing general and specific professional development sessions (Dole, 2004). Still others report that paperwork and administrative tasks consume their time (Dole & Donaldson, 2006). In recent years, as greater emphasis has been placed on the potential of a literacy coach to improve the effectiveness of a school's reading program, recommendations from professional organizations and researchers have helped to clarify the role of the literacy coach.

According to the IRA (2004), the primary responsibilities of the literacy coach should encompass support for the classroom teacher, instruction within and outside the classroom, assessment of student strengths and needs, and leadership both within the school and between the home and school. Literacy coaches also provide professional development for teachers on effective reading practices and culturally informed teaching (Tatum, 2004). This leadership often includes tasks such as selecting reading materials, coordinating the reading program, planning literacy lessons and strategies with teachers, modeling lessons for teachers, and co-teaching.

What Are the Current Recommendations for the Role of the Literacy Coach?

In many school districts, the role of the literacy coach is undefined and ambiguous. Perceptions of literacy coaches vary among the coaches themselves, teachers, and administrators. At a recent gathering, literacy coaches were asked to define their job role as literacy coach as perceived by themselves, teachers, and school administrators. When asked to explain how others define their job responsibilities, coaches offered a myriad of responses: lesson modeler, classroom researcher, resource provider, change agent, assessment analyzer, purchasing agent, student advocate, literacy program implementation police, principal's spy, learner, substitute teacher, book study leader, grade-level facilitator, trainer, and supervisor.

While we agree with several of these perceptions (change agent, learner, student advocate), we strongly disagree with others (implementation police, principal's spy, supervisor, substitute teacher). Literacy coaching has the best chance for success when the role of literacy coach is clearly defined. In this section, we propose our list of job roles for the literacy coach. These job roles are illustrated in Figure 1.1.

Coaching Teachers to Plan for Instruction

Effective literacy instruction is not simply a matter of selecting a commercial reading program and then following the instructions in the teachers' manual (Au, 2002). Effective teachers must be knowledgeable and reflective about literacy research and instructional practices, and they must use that knowledge to make informed instructional decisions that will meet the literacy learning needs of students. Teaching is "systematic presentation of content assumed necessary for mastery within a general area of knowledge" (Algozzine & Ysseldyke, 2006, p. 7). Effective teachers plan, manage,

Figure 1.1 Job Roles of the Literacy Coach

deliver, and evaluate their content presentations. Through ongoing collaboration and problem solving, literacy coaches can help teachers to effectively implement each of these instructional components.

VOICES FROM THE FIELD

"It was awkward when I first became a literacy coach because I went from being a teacher to being a literacy coach at the same school. So, I was somehow viewed differently from my friends. When I first went into classrooms, my friends would want to gossip about peers or the administration. I really had to resist this. I remember that I had to literally write down what my responsibilities were as a literacy coach. So, I sat down with each teacher and explained the purpose of my job and how I was there to really help teachers within their own classrooms. I think this helped with communication. Teachers started to realize that I was there for a real purpose. We all got on the same page about my role as a literacy coach."

Terry

Effective planning involves making decisions about what content to teach, how to teach it, and how to communicate realistic teaching expectations to students. Each of these decisions includes specific activities that can be supported by effective coaching.

Coaches help teachers decide *what to teach* by assessing students' skills, analyzing the instructional task, establishing a logical instructional sequence, considering contextual variables, analyzing instructional groupings, and identifying gaps between actual and expected performance. Deciding *how to teach* means setting instructional goals, selecting instructional methods and materials, pacing instruction appropriately, monitoring performance, and revising instruction. Examples of coaching activities related to helping teachers plan instruction in both early childhood (preK–K) and elementary classrooms (Grades 1–3) classrooms can be found in Table 1.1.

Coaching Teachers to Develop Manageable Classrooms

Managing includes preparing for instruction, using time productively, and creating a positive environment. Each of these decisions includes specific activities that can be supported by effective coaching.

Literacy coaches help teachers prepare for instruction by helping them set and communicate classroom rules, teach consequences of behavior, handle disruptions effectively and efficiently, and teach student self-management skills. Literacy coaches and teachers work collaboratively to establish routines and procedures, organize the physical space, create transitions that are brief, limit interruptions, and allocate sufficient time to academic content instruction. Creating a positive environment means making classrooms friendly places, accepting individual differences, keeping interactions positive, and involving all students in all classroom activities (Algozzine & Ysseldyke, 2006).

Preparing for instruction, using time productively, and creating a positive environment are important aspects of effective teaching. Examples of coaching activities related to helping teachers manage these areas of instruction in early childhood (preK–K) and elementary classrooms (Grades 1–3) can be found in Table 1.2.

Coaching Teachers to Deliver Effective Instruction

Delivering instruction involves presenting content, monitoring student learning, and adjusting instruction. Each of these decisions includes specific activities that can be supported by effective coaching.

Table 1.1   Helping Teachers Plan Instruction in PreK–K and Grades 1–3

Activity	*Coaching Example*
Decide What to Teach	*Work collaboratively with the teacher to*
• assess students' skills	• *ask children to name uppercase letters* • *ask children to answer comprehension questions*
• analyze instructional tasks	• *identify instructional strategies for developing sound-letter connections* • *identify instructional strategies for developing prosody when reading aloud*
• establish logical instruction	• *list the sequence of steps for a rhyming game* • *list the sequence of steps for a making-words activity*
• consider context variables	• *identify children's familiarity with the alphabet system* • *identify children's access to reading materials at home*
• analyze instructional groups	• *establish small groups for learning center time* • *establish guided reading groups based on students' reading levels*
• identify performance gaps	• *analyze assessment data to determine students' knowledge of print concepts* • *analyze assessment data to determine students' vocabulary knowledge*
Decide How to Teach	*Work collaboratively with the teacher to*
• set instructional goals	• *identify goals for phonemic awareness acquisition* • *identify goals for fluency development*
• select methods and materials	• *organize materials for a phonemic awareness lesson* • *select texts for an oral reading lesson*
• pace instruction appropriately	• *establish a timeline for presenting phonemic awareness lessons* • *establish a timeline for rehearsal of a Reader's Theater script*
• monitor performance and revise	• *based on observations of student performance, revise lessons on letter identification* • *based on observations of student performance, revise preparations for Reader's Theater presentations*

(Continued)

Table 1.1 (Continued)

Activity	*Coaching Example*
Communicate Expectations	*Work collaboratively with the teacher to*
• actively involve students	• *establish a routine for students as they listen and respond to a read aloud*
	• *establish a routine for students as they participate in a literature circle*
• explicitly state expectations	• *explain expectations for students' participation during a read aloud*
	• *explain the role of each student as a literature circle participant*
• maintain high standards	• *monitor appropriate listening behaviors during read alouds*
	• *monitor the interaction of students during literature circles*

Literacy coaches work with teachers to present lessons that are relevant to their students. Students need experiences in the classroom that develop their reading and writing processes, show how reading and writing are necessary in their lives, and develop their independence as readers and writers. These lessons must maintain student attention, communicate goals of instruction, and check for student understanding. Coaches help teachers develop instruction that is engaging, motivational, and purposeful in the lives of their students.

Presenting content, monitoring student learning, and adjusting instruction are important aspects of effective teaching. Examples of coaching activities related to helping teachers deliver instruction in early childhood (preK–K) and elementary classrooms (Grades 1–3) can be found in Table 1.3.

Fostering a Collaborative Professional Environment

Literacy coaches must create and maintain a supportive professional collaboration with teachers. The teacher-coach relationship is reciprocal: teachers learn from coaches, coaches learn from teachers, and both learn from students. These close collaborations help to establish a positive learning environment for all members of the school community. Effective literacy coaches foster these collaborative environments by encouraging teachers to share their insights, knowledge, beliefs, and experiences during coaching conversations and professional

Table 1.2   Helping Teachers Manage Instruction in PreK–K and Grades 1–3

Activity	*Coaching Example*
Prepare for Instruction	*Work collaboratively with the teacher to*
• set and communicate rules	• *establish rules for student behavior during center time* • *establish rules for student behavior during independent work time*
• teach consequences of behavior	• *establish a system for acknowledging appropriate student behavior* • *establish a system for responding to inappropriate student behavior*
• handle disruptions efficiently	• *establish a plan for responding to inappropriate student behavior in whole group settings* • *establish a plan for responding to inappropriate student behavior in small group settings*
• teach students self-management	• *develop questions to ask of students as they prepare to transition from one center to another* • *develop a list of questions for students to use when self-assessing their written work*
Use Time Productively	*Work collaboratively with the teacher to*
• establish routines and procedures	• *identify current routines that are ineffective* • *establish a routine for independent reading time*
• organize physical space	• *organize the classroom library* • *organize the writing center*
• keep transitions brief	• *identify ways to reduce transition time from one center to another* • *identify ways to reduce transition time from independent activities to whole group activities*
• limit interruptions	• *identify options for students who need help completing a learning center task* • *list options for students who complete assigned work early*
• use an academic, task-oriented focus	• *identify the components student must include in a rhyming activity* • *identify the components students must include in a persuasive letter*
• allocate sufficient time to academics	• *establish a timetable for introducing theme-based vocabulary concepts* • *plan a week-long literacy block*

(Continued)

Table 1.2 (Continued)

Activity	Coaching Example
Create a Positive Environment	*Work collaboratively with the teacher to*
• make the classroom a friendly place	• *begin each morning meeting with an engaging rhyme or song*
	• *encourage behaviors that are mutually respectful*
• accept individual differences	• *read literature related to valuing individual differences*
	• *discuss appropriate responses to students who present their writing during author's chair time*
• keep interactions positive	• *identify ways to provide supportive feedback to students*
	• *model a positive tone when responding to student questions*
• involve students	• *acknowledge supportive interactions between students*
	• *identify ways in which students can provide supportive feedback to one another*

development sessions. Understanding the foundations of effective teaching is the first step in helping teachers to refine their instructional practice. Understanding how teachers use and interact with their models and mentors to improve their instructional practice is a critical next step for literacy coaches.

At the core of every outstanding preservice apprenticeship program is a commitment to provide a practical foundation for future teaching through field experiences that demonstrate proven, established, and successful strategies for teaching reading—and a mentoring relationship that involves regular debriefing of fieldwork activities for greater understanding and future effectiveness in the classroom. These same principles apply to effective coaching relationships.

In *Teaching Reading Well*, the IRA (2007) provided a synthesis of research on teacher preparation for reading instruction. In college and university preparation programs, field teaching provides preservice teachers with practical experience in using their newly acquired knowledge and skills to assess student needs and to plan, manage, deliver, and evaluate lessons under direct and indirect supervision. The leaders of these programs pair students with experienced teachers who act as models, and they put them in classrooms that are as

Table 1.3   Helping Teachers Deliver Instruction in PreK–K and Grades 1–3

Activity	*Coaching Example*
Present Content	*Work collaboratively with the teacher to*
• present lessons	• *implement an integrated phonics lesson*
	• *implement a lesson on making inferences*
• make lessons relevant	• *identify relevant background knowledge that students bring to a unit of study*
	• *connect new concepts to students' own experiences*
• maintain student attention	• *engage students in kinesthetic activities that relate to sound-letter connections*
	• *engage students in peer interactions to facilitate text comprehension*
• communicate goals of instruction	• *explain the rationale for a phonics activity*
	• *write lesson objectives where students can see them*
• check student understanding	• *ask comprehension questions throughout the presentation of a lesson*
	• *ask students to recap directions before they begin independent work*
• teach thinking skills	• *ask questions that encourage students to connect new information to their own experiences*
	• *use strategies, such as a discussion web, that require students to consider different points of view*
• teach learning strategies	• *teach students to look for phonograms when trying to decipher an unfamiliar word*
	• *teach students to use the five-finger rule when selecting a book for independent reading*
• show enthusiasm	• *model an interest in different genres*
	• *use library resources to research topics with students*
• assign interesting work	• *identify age-appropriate topics for unit studies*
	• *use a variety of sources to teach literacy skills in context*
• use rewards intermittently	• *list rewards currently used; then list other ways to respond positively to student effort*
	• *develop alternatives to external reward routines*
• assign work that students can achieve	• *identify the progression of writing process stages*
	• *determine students' reading levels*

(Continued)

Table 1.3 (Continued)

Activity	*Coaching Example*
• teach skills to mastery	• *scaffold instruction so that phonics skills are presented in multiple contexts* • *provide multiple opportunities for students to make inferences*
• vary instructional materials	• *list potential materials for tactile letter formation* • *acquire different types of texts for a classroom library*
Monitor Student Learning	*Work collaboratively with the teacher to*
• give feedback	• *identify for students those elements that make their work effective* • *conference with individual students about their independent reading*
• actively engage students	• *ask for student input about their work on a project* • *establish a student self-assessment tool for written work*
• redirect students not responding	• *rephrase a question to which a student is not responding* • *review concepts that may connect to new material*
• provide ways to request help	• *list with students ways in which they can request help* • *list sources to which students can turn to answer their questions*
Adjust Instruction	*Work collaboratively with the teacher to*
• vary teaching approaches	• *identify the readability levels of different texts* • *identify and apply alternative strategies for fluency instruction*
• vary materials	• *use a different medium for presenting literacy concepts* • *establish a balance in terms of fiction and nonfiction text use*
• vary pace	• *establish options for inviting oral language use* • *revise the guided reading routine based on student needs*

typical of contemporary educational settings as possible. They provide them with carefully arranged, hands-on demonstrations of effective instructional methods, and they provide corrective and supportive feedback as their students teach and practice what they have learned. The overall goal is to provide supervised opportunities to teach that mirror and reinforce the course work and preparation provided in the university and field settings. The best practices in teaching teachers—explicit explanation and demonstration of content, and high levels of active and engaged responding with feedback, followed by multiple practice opportunities, continuous evaluation of progress, and adjustment of instruction—turn out to be the best practices in preschool and elementary school classrooms.

Teacher educators know that two factors influence the success of field experiences: opportunities to practice in classrooms where references to course and case content are explicit; and guidance from master teachers, with ongoing feedback to support effective and correct ineffective teaching behaviors (Maheady, Mallette, & Harper, 1996; Mallette, Maheady, & Harper, 1999; Mallette, Kile, Smith, McKinney, & Readence, 2000).

Similarly, effective coaching relationships are built on principles and practices of effective teaching practices, fostered through collaborative professional environments, which promote thinking through reflective inquiry and allow student data to guide instructional decisions. In this way, coaching is designed to reinforce practices and help teachers become more aware and intentional about their teaching. It triggers needed reflection on the reasons behind use of a particular approach to reach students. Teachers develop knowledge that is established, ingrained, and extended with real-world applications in the classroom.

The most effective coaches provide frequent and continuous support in the teacher's classroom to help turn knowledge and principles into effective teaching practices. Guided demonstrations in real-time classrooms are a key factor in establishing sustained changes in teaching behavior (IRA, 2007). Providing support to practicing teachers means opening up their instructional spaces so they can ask questions and make multiple attempts with different instructional approaches, and the process must include a system of observations and guided feedback.

Promoting Thinking Through Reflective Inquiry

Effective literacy coaches encourage teachers to think reflectively about their practice. That is, literacy coaches hold mirrors to teachers in hopes that teachers will *re-see* the instructional decisions they made and whether these were effective decisions for their students. The coach serves as a guide and mentor, but the essential insight comes from within the teacher.

Effective literacy coaches encourage teachers to think deeply about their instructional practice, question decisions they make, find evidence that their instruction is impacting students, and consider how their teaching can be improved.

Allowing Student Data to Guide Instructional Decisions

Evaluation, discussed at length in Chapter 4, is the process teachers use to determine whether their teaching is effective. Sometimes they use formative evaluation to make decisions while they are teaching, and other times they make decisions after they have taught. Six activities contribute to evaluating effectively: monitoring students' understanding, monitoring engaged time, maintaining records of students' progress, informing students about their progress, using data to make decisions, and making judgments about students' performance (Algozzine & Ysseldyke, 2006). Examples of coaching activities related to helping teachers evaluate instruction in early childhood (preK–K) and elementary classrooms (Grades 1–3) can be found in Table 1.4.

What Are the Qualities of Effective Literacy Coaches?

Literacy coaches are as diverse as the teachers they lead. Some are quiet but poignant. Others are assertive but collaborative. Regardless of their personality type, there are common traits among literacy coaches who dedicate themselves to helping teachers fulfill the literacy mission of the school and enrich the literacy lives of their students. Effective literacy coaches

- are content experts
- are collaborative advisors and confidants
- honor the knowledge of the teacher

Content Experts

Literacy coaches are knowledgeable of literacy processes. Often, this knowledge comes from an advanced degree in a literacy-related

Table 1.4   Helping Teachers Evaluate Instruction in PreK–K and
Grades 1–3

Activity	*Coaching Example*
Monitor Understanding	*Work collaboratively with the teacher to*
• check understanding of directions	• *observe students' implementation of multistep directions*
	• *ask students to explain directions to a partner*
	• *establish checkpoints within a lesson*
• check process students use to do work	• *use a writing conference to assess student progress*
• check success rates	• *analyze the degree to which a student correctly identifies rhyming words*
	• *list frequent misspellings found in a student's work*
Monitor Engaged Time	*Work collaboratively with the teacher to*
• ensure active engagement	• *incorporate an element of student choice in particular center activities*
	• *use small groups to facilitate participation among all students*
• self-monitor teaching performance	• *reflect on the progress of a small group rhyming lesson*
	• *identify ways in which student participation in a vocabulary lesson can be increased*
	• *observe students' behavior as a lesson proceeds*
• scan for engagement	• *observe students' body language and facial expression as signals of engagement*
Maintain Records	*Work collaboratively with the teacher to*
• keep up-to-date scores of performance	• *establish a way to monitor students' participation in centers*
• chart student progress	• *establish a way to compile and organize samples of student work*
	• *establish a schedule for assessing students' knowledge of sound-letter correspondence*
	• *establish a way to record students' independent reading selections*
Inform Students About Progress	*Work collaboratively with the teacher to*
• provide feedback	• *respond to students' input about a story*
	• *identify areas of improvement in student writing*

(Continued)

Table 1.4 (Continued)

Activity	Coaching Example
• correct errors	• model the use of conventional spelling, while encouraging students' attempts to write using transitional spelling • ask students to correct their misspellings of high-frequency words that have been taught in class
• provide general and specific praise	• praise a group of students for their efforts during meeting time • tell a student why his or her response to text was insightful
• encourage self-correction	• answer a student's question with a question that will encourage the student to problem solve • identify self-correction strategies that students can use independently
Use Data to Make Decisions	Work collaboratively with the teacher to
• decide when to refer for assistance	• identify patterns in a student's speech that may require help from a specialist • invite appropriate school personnel to observe a student's group interactions
• make teaching changes	• review concepts of print based on analysis of assessment data • use interactive strategies to improve students' inferential comprehension skills
• decide when to stop special assistance	• confer regularly with the intervention specialist about a student's progress • analyze student work samples to identify patterns of improvement
Make Judgments About Performance	Work collaboratively with the teacher to
• specify continuing goals for students	• involve parents in goal setting and offer ideas for home-school connections • use student input to establish reasonable goals
• chart progress	• maintain anecdotal records of students' oral language development • chart students' fluency progress in terms of accuracy, automaticity, and prosody

graduate program. In some cases, literacy coaches without advanced degrees have had ongoing professional development experiences that have enriched their literacy knowledge and prepared them for their role as literacy coach. Regardless, credible literacy coaches are ones who know how young children develop and thrive as readers and writers.

For teachers to gain insight about literacy, they must have confidence that their coaches are knowledgeable about reading and writing instruction. Literacy coaches must instill in their teachers, who in turn will instill in their students, that literacy learning is a lifelong process. In this respect, literacy coaches must constantly strive to enrich their own literacy knowledge by reading professional books, research and teacher-oriented journal articles, and Web sites and newsletters of professional organizations such as the IRA, the National Council of Teachers of English, and the National Association for the Education of Young Children.

Literacy is not a stagnant field of inquiry. New research emerges every day that tells a fuller, more complicated picture of how young children best learn to read and write. One of the most important qualities literacy coaches must have is a desire to constantly build their content expertise and inspire their teachers to do the same. In doing so, coaches can more effectively link the reading program of a school to the broader literacy goals established by a state or school district (Shanklin, 2006).

VOICES FROM THE FIELD

"When I meet with teachers, I explain to them my role from the perspective of a basketball coach. For example, Michael Jordan went to the University of North Carolina and was coached by Dean Smith. I ask my teachers, 'Who was a better basketball player: Michael Jordan or Dean Smith?' Naturally, the teachers reply, 'Michael Jordan.' Yes, of course, but Dean Smith coached him. So, I explain to teachers that I am not there to say that I am a better teacher than they are. But, as a coach, I have the luxury of observing and analyzing just like Dean Smith did. Like Dean Smith, I hope to bring out the best in the teachers. When I make this analogy to the teachers, I think they get a better sense of my job role."

Sarah

Collaborative Advisors and Confidants

When literacy coaches enter classrooms, some teachers respond with trepidation and suspicion. Teachers want to improve the quality of their teaching, but they fear the judgmental eyes of others who enter their room. In this regard, literacy coaches are *collaborative confidants*. Together, they work with teachers to learn about students, but do so in ways that promote collaboration between the teacher and coach in a nonevaluative manner. Even during challenges or setbacks, the coach must remain discrete and supportive—careful to respect both the individual differences and the professional needs of each teacher (Shanklin, 2006).

Effective literacy coaches understand that the relationship they establish with teachers is critical in helping the teacher grow as a professional. When coaches talk about their teachers to other teaching colleagues or to the principal, they undermine this relationship. For literacy coaches to be effective, teachers must believe that their coach will always support them and use discretion. Whether a teacher is hopeful or worried, confident or confused, the coach and teacher can work collaboratively to build on the teacher's strengths and to refine instructional practices that are in need of improvement. When coaches serve as nonthreatening advisors, they listen to the successes and challenges of the teacher, participate in the celebrations, sympathize with the struggles, and gently guide teachers toward self-reflection and continued inquiry.

Knowledge Acknowledgers

Literacy coaches are not the only experts in the classroom. During coaching conversations, teachers express their own valuable knowledge, experience, and expertise. Whether they are beginners or veterans in the field, the teachers' experience matters and informs conversations between literacy coach and teacher. Effective literacy coaches recognize, and are not threatened by, the wealth of knowledge teachers bring to the conversation. Literacy coaches should encourage teachers to offer opinions, insights, and experiences during coaching sessions. When coaches acknowledge the important insights their teachers offer, they effectively build confidence and rapport.

Today, the literacy coach's responsibilities can be as varied as the teaching contexts in which they work. Fulfilling the promise of literacy coaching is particularly challenging given the changing nature of the role and the variability with which those changes have been communicated to different groups, particularly to administrators and teachers. We believe, however, that it is a challenge worth undertaking. A basic premise of the No Child Left Behind Act that drives the educational policy in the United States today is that every public school classroom will have a "qualified teacher." Colleges and universities play a role in achieving this goal, but coaches working in real-life classrooms with practicing teachers play a more important part in making this happen and in sustaining it over time.

Next Steps: Professional Development Suggestions

1. Working with a group of literacy coaches from different schools, discuss how the role of the literacy coach has evolved in each of your schools. Describe how those changes in role were communicated to teachers and administrators. Brainstorm ways to facilitate this process more effectively.

2. Using the activities and actions listed in Tables 1.1, 1.2, 1.3, and 1.4, collaborate with individual teachers to prioritize these actions in terms of their own professional development needs. Then, list ways in which you as the literacy coach can support them in each of the identified areas.

3. Working with other literacy coaches, discuss ways in which you support teachers in addressing each of the activities and actions listed in Tables 1.1, 1.2, 1.3, and 1.4.

4. Using Table 1.5 as a guide, survey the teachers and administrators in your school about their perceptions of and expectations for the role of the literacy coach. Based on the results, discuss ways in which your role can be clarified and, if necessary, refined to meet the needs of the teachers and students.

Table 1.5   Survey of Roles and Expectations for Literacy Coaching

Listed below are some of the activities in which a literacy coach may engage, based on the recommendations of Bean (2004). In the first column (1) after each statement, indicate the degree to which you believe that activity is a current part of the literacy coach's role, with 1 being "not a significant part of the coach's role" and 5 being "a highly significant part of the coach's role." In the second column (2) after each statement, indicate the degree to which you think that activity needs to be part of the coach's role, with 1 being "does not need to be part of the coach's role" and 5 being "should definitely be part of the coach's role."

Statement	(1) Is this currently part of the coach's role?	(2) Should this be part of the coach's role?
1. Talks with colleagues about relevant issues or needs	1 2 3 4 5	1 2 3 4 5
2. Recommends materials for literacy instruction	1 2 3 4 5	1 2 3 4 5
3. Works with colleagues on curriculum development	1 2 3 4 5	1 2 3 4 5
4. Participates with colleagues in professional development activities such as workshops or conferences	1 2 3 4 5	1 2 3 4 5
5. Leads or participates in study groups with teachers	1 2 3 4 5	1 2 3 4 5
6. Assesses students	1 2 3 4 5	1 2 3 4 5
7. Instructs students	1 2 3 4 5	1 2 3 4 5
8. Assists teachers with lesson planning	1 2 3 4 5	1 2 3 4 5
9. Holds grade-level team meetings	1 2 3 4 5	1 2 3 4 5
10. Analyzes student work	1 2 3 4 5	1 2 3 4 5
11. Helps teachers to interpret assessment data	1 2 3 4 5	1 2 3 4 5
12. Talks with individual teachers about instructional issues	1 2 3 4 5	1 2 3 4 5
13. Leads professional development presentations for teachers	1 2 3 4 5	1 2 3 4 5
14. Models lessons	1 2 3 4 5	1 2 3 4 5
15. Co-teaches lessons	1 2 3 4 5	1 2 3 4 5
16. Observes teachers teaching and provides feedback	1 2 3 4 5	1 2 3 4 5

2

The Nuts and Bolts

Scheduling, Organizing, and Documenting

(with Paola Pilonieta)

In this chapter, we offer suggestions to literacy coaches for scheduling, organizing, and documenting during different phases of the school year:

- Before the school year begins
  - o determining your role
  - o gathering information
  - o gathering professional resources

- At the beginning of the school year
  - o introducing yourself
  - o setting up an office
  - o record keeping
  - o scheduling time
  - o managing materials

- During the school year
  - o working one-on-one with teachers
  - o working with groups

- Wrapping up the school year
  - o inventorying materials
  - o closing the current year's files

Each phase of the school year brings forth unique challenges, and this means that shifting your focus is important. As with any job, proper organization and planning will help you transition smoothly across different times of the year. Being prepared will also assist you in being regarded as a professional by the teachers and administrators in your school. This may be of particular importance if you are working as a literacy coach in a school where you were once a classroom teacher.

Before the School Year Begins: Making the Most of Summer Vacation

In Chapter 1, we pointed out that there is no single, clear-cut job description for literacy coaches (Hall, 2004; International Reading Association, 2004); in fact, responsibilities vary from state to state, from district to district, and even from school to school. For example, some districts hire school-based literacy coaches, while others have traveling coaches. School-based literacy coaches work with the teachers in only one school and may have a wider role and scope of responsibilities. Along with working with teachers (observing, planning, and modeling lessons), they may also be asked to manage reading materials for students, analyze high-stakes reading test scores, plan professional development sessions, coordinate tutoring programs, and order new materials. Instead of working with just one school, traveling literacy coaches work with a target group of teachers (preschool teachers, primary teachers, or novice teachers) in several schools and may be asked to perform some of the duties of school-based literacy coaches.

Determining Your Role

VOICES FROM THE FIELD

"I wish I had known how hard it can be working with a bunch of different teachers. There can be so many ups and downs in one day. You can go from having a really positive experience in one classroom to a really negative experience an hour later in another classroom. You just have to prepare yourself for all the different personalities you will encounter in one day."

Sam

Once you know what type of literacy coach you will be, it is important to meet with your supervisor and decide what your responsibilities will be. If you are a school-based literacy coach, your supervisor will most likely be the principal. If you are a traveling literacy coach, your supervisor may be a more experienced literacy coach responsible for coordinating the activities of several literacy coaches in the district. In either case, this is the time to discuss expectations and goals for the school year: "if the reading coaches are to be successful in promoting changes in classroom practices, the expectations for the role of reading coach need to be clear and understood by both the reading coaches and the school administrator" (International Reading Association, 2004, p. 4). Below is a list of questions that you may want to ask your supervisor. The answers to these questions will be instrumental in planning out your school year.

- With which teachers will I be working?
- When and how frequently will I meet with the school administrator to whom I report?
- What resources (both monetary and in terms of staff) do I have at my disposal?
- What are your goals in the area of literacy for your students?
- What are your goals for the teachers?
- What is your overall literacy mission for the school?
- What literacy programs do you currently use in your school/district?
- Are there any supplemental programs being used? If so, what are they?
- Are there schoolwide, districtwide, or statewide programs or assessment protocols of which I should be aware?
- Will I be part of student evaluation committees (e.g., special education, English learner placement)?
- How do you envision my role as a literacy coach?

To develop your background knowledge of the school and district, you should also find the answers to the questions below. You should be able to locate the answers to these questions on the school's or district's Web pages; however, if you can't find the answers there, you may want to ask your supervisor or colleagues.

- What is your school's/district's population like in terms of race, ethnicity, socioeconomic status, and English language learners (ELLs)?

- Is there a particular challenge facing your school/district (e.g., recent change in demographics, meeting new certification standards, a mobile student population, or large staff turnover)?
- What was your school's performance on the state's high-stakes test? If schools are ranked or graded according to performance on this test, what is your school's grade or rank?
- What are your school's AYP (adequate yearly progress) goals?
- Do I need any passwords to access district databases or software programs?

Gathering Information

When we close our eyes and imagine our summer vacation, it is sometimes hard to picture ourselves reading through journals, going through textbooks, or sitting in front of the computer. This may, however, be the perfect time to start gathering professional resources and learning about programs in your new school (see the appendix).

Becoming Familiar With Your School or District

You want to start the school year as prepared as possible. One way to do this is to do as much background research as you can before commencing your day-to-day responsibilities as a literacy coach. Start with a self-assessment. Are you familiar with all of the schools' literacy programs, supplemental programs, literacy initiatives, and assessment protocols? If not, now is the time to learn.

If you are joining a program that heavily relies on various statewide assessments to guide instruction and target students for remediation and you are unfamiliar with these assessment tools, use the time before school begins to attend training workshops offered by your district. If none are being offered, look for information in literacy journals or the Internet. If you are not affiliated with or near a university or don't have access to an academic database, Google Scholar (http://scholar.google.com/) is a valuable resource. As the name implies, this search engine helps you find more scholarly information on educational topics. You can often download journal articles and chapters, and preview books free of charge. Colleagues can also be a great source of information.

Gathering Professional Resources

Based on your findings from conversations with teachers and administrators, begin to establish priorities for the school year ahead.

Investigate topics that are new to you. Identify specific challenges faced by your school or district. Start collecting instructional strategies, ideas, and Web sites that you could potentially share with teachers. You can create a binder for each of these topics and fill it with articles, strategies, and Web sites for each goal with which you are working. For example, if your colleagues are concerned about meeting the needs of an increasing ELL population, you may want to create a binder with tabs and organize it in the following manner:

- Introductory information: In this section, you may want to have articles and chapters that introduce teachers and support staff to the special needs and challenges that can be encountered when working with ELLs.
- Strategies: In this section, you may want to include articles, chapters, and ideas that discuss specific strategies that can be used with ELL students. Include any modifications that can be made to the strategy for students with learning disabilities. This section can be further subdivided by grade: strategies appropriate for prekindergarten and kindergarten, and those best suited for first and second grades.
- Assessments: Here, you can include information on assessment tools, rubrics, and other evaluation instruments that teachers can use to help them measure ELLs' progress.
- Web sites: In this section, you can include Web sites that teachers can use to help them develop their knowledge about ELL students. You can also include Web sites the children can use to gain proficiency in the target skill. In both cases, you should include a brief description of the Web site and the material that can be found there.
- Student work samples: Here, you may want to include pictures or actual artifacts of students' work. These should be samples of strategies that you have introduced from your "strategies" section in the notebook. In this way, when you conduct future professional development workshops, you can have examples of students experiencing success by using the strategy you are highlighting. Seeing these examples may encourage other teachers to try the strategy.
- Agendas: You will need to create an agenda for any professional development workshop you conduct. Once you have provided the workshop, you may want to make notes to yourself about improvements that can be made the next time you present this session. For example, you may note that you need

to allocate more time for discussion, or that the article used to introduce the material was not as useful as you had hoped. These notes will assist you in planning subsequent workshops on this topic.

- Committee assignments: In this section, you should include information pertaining to any committees to which you have been assigned. Include contact information for committee members, criteria for placement into the programs, and a breakdown of who qualifies for services.
- Courses of study: You should have the state and local curriculum standards for each grade with which you work.

Having a solid plan and taking time to prepare for your new job can save you a lot of time later on during the school year. Focus your preparation along three major areas: (1) communicating with your supervisor to define your role and responsibilities, (2) acquiring background knowledge about your school or school district, and (3) gathering professional resources that meet the specific needs of your school or district.

At the Beginning of the School Year

The beginning of the year is a busy time, and it is easy to feel overwhelmed when you think about all of the things you have to do. This next section will guide you as you introduce yourself to your coworkers, set up your office, schedule your time, and manage your materials. Careful planning and organization can help you to establish an effective framework for your work with colleagues throughout the school year.

Introducing Yourself

Once the teachers return to school to prepare for the new academic year, it will be time to introduce yourself to them. Your principal may do this during the first faculty meeting; you may even be asked to kick off the school year with a workshop for the entire faculty. Before doing so, it may also be helpful to send a letter or e-mail to the teachers with whom you will be working. This will give you the opportunity to describe your role in more detail, explain your teaching background (e.g., grades taught, number of years teaching, educational credentials), and introduce the services you will be providing and the resources you will have available for teachers. It is also important to think about word choice for the letter as this can set the tone for future relationships. How will you address the teachers? *Dear friends* may be too informal and premature; *Dear teachers* may come across to the faculty as if you see yourself above them. Figure 2.1 is a sample letter you can modify to meet your needs.

You can also introduce yourself during grade-level meetings. This can provide you a more informal setting to get to know the teachers at your school. This can also help you get a sense of how the teachers work as a team and issues they may be encountering.

Setting Up Your Office

Depending on your school's resources, the word *office* may be misleading. Your base of operations may be a revamped storage closet. If you are a traveling literacy coach, your "office" could very well be the trunk of your car! In any case, there are some supplies that will help you get organized and start you on the right track.

Figure 2.1   Sample Letter of Introduction

August 15

Dear Colleagues,

Welcome to the start of a new school year! My name is Lucy Colemedina and I have been hired as the new literacy coach for our school. Before coming to Kendall Lakes Elementary School, I taught first grade for seven years at Carver Elementary and third grade for three years at Pinecrest Elementary. During that time I was fortunate to get a master's degree in reading from The State University.

My role as a literacy coach will be to work with you to help our students reach their literacy goals. My role is multifaceted: I will be offering support via grade-level planning meetings, strategy demonstration lessons, classroom observations, professional development sessions, and one-on-one meetings. I invite you to come and discuss these opportunities further. My office is located next to the library in Room 32.

In addition, through support from our parent-teacher organization, we have been able to compile various professional resources for you and your students. Please come explore these in Room 19.

I look forward to a school year filled with collaboration and learning.

Sincerely,

Lucy Colemedina

- Color-coded files: These can be used to file away assessments, strategies, and ideas. You can use the colors to help you differentiate between grades (e.g., red for materials best suited for prekindergarten and kindergarten, green for Grades 1 and 2) or to differentiate between literacy areas (e.g., red for phonemic awareness, orange for phonics, blue for fluency, purple for writing).

- Large three-ring binders and dividers: These binders can serve several purposes. Instead of using file folders, you can organize literacy information in a binder (such as the ELL example offered on pp. 29–30). You can also have a binder to keep track of the teachers with whom you are working. You can have a divider for each teacher that includes their schedule, a class roster, a copy of their needs assessment form, a log of your interactions with them, and observations conducted.

- A rolling cart: Since you will frequently be working in other people's classrooms, you should bring any items you will need to use when modeling lessons or co-teaching. These may include a set of dry-erase markers and an eraser; transparency markers and blank transparencies; chalk and a chalkboard eraser; markers, pens, and pencils; staplers and paper clips; magnets and blue painter's tape to hang charts or posters; name tags; and a timer to maintain the pace of the lesson.

- Digital camera and/or video recorder: Although not mandatory, these items can be very useful to you as a literacy coach. When it is not possible to keep students' work, a photograph can be taken and then used during a workshop to illustrate the results of a strategy. The video recorder can be used to tape yourself or a teacher while conducting a lesson. These tapes can later be used during professional development sessions: "by videotaping strategies that teachers are effectively practicing in their classrooms, the coach can produce compelling evidence of best practices at work" (Blachowicz, Obrochta, & Fogelberg, 2005, p. 58). Once you have videotaped a lesson, you and the teacher can sit together and analyze that lesson.

- General office supplies: You will need pens, highlighters, adhesive notes, adhesive flags (to mark articles in journals or chapters in books), scissors, tape, glue sticks, correction fluid, stapler, paper clips, and a calendar.

Record Keeping

A needs assessment, such as those described in Chapter 6, is a useful tool for beginning the school year and setting goals for the months ahead. You can administer such an assessment during a faculty meeting, attach it to your letter of introduction, or deliver it personally during grade-level meetings. Compiling this information will help you develop an overview of the faculty's strengths and weaknesses and can help you decide what workshops to plan and conduct. Figure 2.2 is an example of a simple form for a needs assessment. The first four questions should be answered by the teacher, and the action plan should be filled out by you in conjunction with the teacher.

Once you have met with all of the teachers about their needs assessment, you can compile the information onto one form (see Figures 2.3 and 2.4). This will give you a handy summary sheet that you can use to keep track of your progress. You can also use this form as a quick guide when meeting with your principal to inform him or her of the work you have been doing.

In your new role, you will be working with different teachers on different instructional aspects. If you are working with several different schools, the task can seem even more daunting. It is important to keep thorough records of your activities. This will help you keep track of your progress with each individual teacher. When meeting with your supervisor, you can also use these logs to document your time.

The design of these logs may depend on the types of activities in which you engage; however, they should all provide an accurate description of the work you do with teachers. If you are working with various schools, you may add a line to the form where you write down the teacher's school. Figure 2.5 is an example of a record-keeping log. Figure 2.6 is an example of how these logs can be filled out. This form should be kept in your grade-level binder. Every time you meet with a teacher to discuss an instructional issue or a student's progress, you should record it on this form. You should also record meetings that were canceled or attempts you have made to schedule an appointment. This is particularly important with teachers who are hesitant to work with you. In this way, you can show your principal that you have made every attempt possible to work with all of your assigned teachers. It will be up to their discretion to decide how to proceed with teachers who are resistant to working with you.

Scheduling Your Time

It is impossible to create a one-size-fits-all scheduling template since each school has its own particular needs and circumstances. We can, however, provide you with some general guidelines you can use to create your own schedule and a sample schedule that illustrates the guidelines.

Figure 2.2 Example of Needs Assessment

Name _____ Date _____

Grade Taught _____

Please answer questions 1–3. I look forward to discussing our Action Plan soon.

1. What are your overall beliefs about teaching literacy?

_____

_____

2. What do you consider to be your strengths as a literacy teacher?

_____

_____

3. In what literacy areas would you like to see your students improve?

_____

_____

_____

4. In what ways can I support you in helping to improve your students' literacy skills?

_____

_____

Action Plan

_____

_____

Figure 2.3   Example Summary of Teachers' Needs

			East Village Elementary 2007–2008				
Teacher	Strengths	Challenges	Coach's Action	Date Taken	Next Steps	Date Taken
Mendez	Classroom management	Fluency	Co-planning	9/15	Team teaching	9/22
Roberts	Guided reading	Comprehension	Lesson modeling	9/17	Co-planning	
Berger	Think alouds	Guided reading	Teacher observation	9/17	Lesson modeling	9/24
Bethel	Phonics	Writing	Team teaching	9/16	Teacher observation	
Hall	Working with ELLs	Vocabulary	Pre-conference	9/15	Lesson modeling	

Figure 2.4 Summary Sheet

Name of School: _____

Teacher	Strengths	Challenges	Coach's Action	Date Taken	Next Steps	Date Taken

Figure 2.5   Sample Record-Keeping Log Template

Coach's Record-Keeping Log

Teacher's Name _____   Grade _____

Date _____   Time _____

Reading Issue Discussed _____

Type of Interaction

_____ Pre-conference   _____ Co-planning   _____ Teacher observation

_____ Team teaching   _____ Lesson modeling   _____ Debriefing meeting

Description of Activity _____

_____

_____

_____

_____

Next Steps _____

_____

_____

_____

_____

(Continued)

Figure 2.5 (Continued)

Date _____   Time _____

Literacy Issue Discussed _____

Type of Interaction

_____ Pre-conference   _____ Co-planning   _____ Teacher observation

_____ Team teaching   _____ Lesson modeling   _____ Debriefing meeting

Description of Activity _____

_____

_____

_____

_____

Next Steps _____

_____

_____

_____

_____

Figure 2.6   Example of Completed Record-Keeping Log

Coach's Record-Keeping Log

Teacher's Name _____Mrs. Farel_____   Grade __2nd__

Date __11/9/07_____ Time ___9:00–9:30_____

Literacy Issue Discussed _____improving fluency_____

Type of Interaction

_____ Pre-conference ___x__ Co-planning _____ Teacher observation

_____ Team teaching _____ Lesson modeling _____ Debriefing meeting

Description of Activity Today we focused on integrating Reader's Theater with the reading lesson. Mrs. Farel will make copies of the Reader's Theater text for the class. Students will be assigned roles and will use their independent reading time to practice. By the end of the week students will take turns performing their Reader's Theater scripts for the class.

Next Steps Our next meeting will be on 11/16. We will hold a debriefing meeting to see how Reader's Theater worked for the students. I will also suggest the possibility of modeling the neurological impress method. She could do this with the students experiencing the most difficulty.

Date __11/16_____ Time ___9:00–9:30_____

Literacy Issue Discussed _____results of Reader's Theater_____

Type of Interaction

_____ Pre-conference _____ Co-planning _____ Teacher observation

_____ Team teaching _____ Lesson modeling ___x___ Debriefing meeting

Description of Activity Mrs. Farel reported that her students enjoyed Reader's Theater. She expressed concern over lack of fluency gains. I explained to her that it might take several weeks before the students made any recordable gains. I also mentioned using the neurological impress method with her students experiencing the most difficulty. She seemed interested in this and I offered to model this strategy the next time we meet.

Next Steps On 11/23 I will model neurological impress method with one of Mrs. Farel's students.

1. Constants: Start by scheduling regular meetings with your supervisor. Some schools have arranged their schedules so that members of the same grades have a common planning time at least once a week. This can be an ideal time for you to provide grade-specific professional development sessions or to work collaboratively as a group in planning and discussing reading issues. If you decide to attend these meetings, block out the time in your schedule. Your district may also have literacy coach meetings where they provide you with further professional development and discuss issues germane to your district. Make sure you block out time for these as well.

2. Meetings: Next, schedule any committee meetings you may have. Be sure to include classroom observations, individualized educational plan meetings, and learning community meetings (see Chapter 5).

3. Planning time: Be sure to set aside time to prepare professional development sessions, attend sessions yourself, and research solutions and alternatives for your teachers.

4. Teacher groupings: Decide how you will work with teachers. Will you work with a few teachers and meet with them frequently and after a predetermined time work with a different group? Or will you work with all of the teachers and meet with them less frequently? Each option has its pros and cons. Meeting frequently with a small group of teachers for approximately six to eight weeks allows you to provide intense support and scaffolding; however, this may only work for short-term goals. Working with all the teachers at once will allow you to address the needs of your teachers sooner, but the support you provide will be less intense and more interspersed. This option may be better suited for goals or changes that require longer periods of time to come about.

Figure 2.7 is a sample schedule of a literacy coach working with one school. Figure 2.8 is a sample schedule of a literacy coach working with multiple schools. This literacy coach works with prekindergarten teachers through second grade teachers, six at each grade. At this school, the principal has arranged the schedule so that each grade has one hour a week to plan collaboratively. During this hour, the teachers discuss special events and curriculum issues. The literacy

Figure 2.7   Sample Schedule for a Literacy Coach at One School

Time	Monday	Tuesday	Wednesday	Thursday	Friday
8:00–10:00	Teacher 1	Teacher 2	Teacher 3	Teacher 4	Literacy coach meetings with teachers, administrators, and parents Literacy coach district meeting and training
10:00–12:00	Teacher 5	Teacher 6	Teacher 7	Teacher 8	
12:00–1:00	Lunch	Lunch	Lunch	Lunch	Coach planning
1:00–3:00	Teacher 9	Teacher 10	Teacher 11	Teacher 12	

coach sits in on these meetings, works with each grade, and sometimes provides a short workshop.

If you are working with multiple schools your schedule may look similar to one for a coach working at a single school (see Figure 2.7) with a few key exceptions. Depending on the number of schools at which you work, you may spend Mondays at School 1, Tuesdays at School 2, and so on. If you are working with more than four or five schools, you may have to spend your mornings at one school and your afternoons at a different school. The scheduling guidelines still apply; however, remember to build in travel time between schools.

Literacy coach schedules will vary greatly depending on the district and school. The schedules included are representative schedules that you will modify to fit your schools' needs. Typically, literacy

Figure 2.8 Sample Schedule for a Literacy Coach at Multiple Schools

Time	Monday School 1	Tuesday School 2	Wednesday School 2	Thursday School 3	Friday
8:00–11:00	Teacher 1	Teacher 2	Teacher 3	Teacher 4	Literacy coach district meeting and training
11:00–12:00	Lunch	Lunch	Lunch	Lunch	Lunch
12:00–3:00	Teacher 5	Teacher 6	Teacher 7	Teacher 8	Coach planning

coaches who work within a single school meet with three to four teachers a day during their literacy block of time. Literacy coaches who travel to different schools typically work in larger blocks of time and with fewer teachers.

Managing Materials

As part of your responsibilities, you may be in charge of supplemental reading materials for students and professional resources for teachers. For students, you may have class sets of trade books or leveled books for guided reading. For teachers, you may have journals, professional books, and videos demonstrating literacy instruction. These materials may be housed in a separate room or in your office.

If your school does not have one already, you will have to develop a procedure for checking out materials and keeping track of the resources. If you have to develop your own system for checking out books, you may wish to begin by using a simple checkout system, similar to the classic library card system. Put a pocket on the back of each book. Inside the pocket add a card (with the book's title) where the interested teacher can write her name and the date. When the teacher wants to check out the book, whether for students or for herself, she pulls out the card from the back of the book, writes her name and the date, and puts the card inside a file box. The file box should have a tab for each teacher's name; that way, it is easy for you to see what books are being checked out and who is checking them out. When the teacher returns the book, she pulls the card from the file box and puts it back inside the book's pocket.

Another idea is to have a checkout log. On this log, teachers write their names, the date, and the names of the books they are checking out. When they return the item, they just add the return date on the log. Figure 2.9 shows an example of this log. Regardless of how you proceed, it is important to have the checkout/check-in procedures clearly posted in the materials room. Eventually, as you acquire additional resources, you may want to consider using a computerized system, similar to those systems used in modern libraries.

If you are working with multiple schools, you probably won't be asked to manage a school's supplemental reading materials; however, you may be asked to distribute materials to the teachers with whom you work. This may be especially true if you are receiving support from a grant. In that case, you may want to create a log similar to the one used for checking out materials. Figure 2.10 is an example of this log. In this way, you will be able to keep track of the materials you distribute, and if there is ever any doubt about a teacher's receiving materials, you can always refer to your log.

The teachers in your school will look to you—the literacy coach—for guidance in addressing their instructional challenges. A thoughtful introduction will help to begin your collaborative work. Having procedures in place for record keeping, scheduling, and managing materials at the start of the school year will allow you to direct more of your attention to improving students' reading achievement.

During the School Year

Once you are organized, it is time to focus on working with teachers. During the year, when providing professional development to teachers, your time will be spent doing two things: working one-on-one and working with groups. In the next section, we describe different models that can be used when working in both individual and group contexts.

Working One-on-One: Coaching Options

- Co-planning: In this situation, the literacy coach and the classroom teacher plan the lesson together. The literacy coach can talk the classroom teacher through the lesson and help her anticipate problematic moments.

Figure 2.9   Sample Material Checkout Log

Material Checkout Log				
Checkout Date	*Teacher's Name*	*Item's Title*	*Quantity*	*Return Date*

Figure 2.10   Sample Distribution Log

Distribution Log				
Item Title	*Quantity*	*Teacher's Name*	*Teacher's Signature*	*Date*

- Co-teaching: As the name implies, this scenario has the literacy coach and the classroom teacher teaching the lesson together. For co-teaching to succeed, the literacy coach and the teacher must meet beforehand to discuss the lesson and decide who will teach what.
- Lesson modeling: This option provides the teacher with the most support. In this scenario, the literacy coach models the strategy while the classroom teacher observes. Afterward, the literacy coach and the teacher meet to discuss the lesson and the literacy coach can clarify any elements of the lesson that may have been confusing.

In addition to the coaching options presented above, meetings and observations are important components of a literacy coach's tool kit.

- Meetings: In the sample record-keeping log in Figure 2.5, you will find pre-conference meetings, debriefing meetings, and follow-up meetings. All of these play an important role in the coaching process. Pre-conference meetings serve to set up goals for the school year and help you decide at which point of the continuum to provide services. Debriefing meetings are extremely important because they help to clarify elements of the lesson and they help to plan the next steps. Follow-up meetings are useful because they occur after the teacher has had the opportunity to use the strategy for a significant period of time. These meetings allow the literacy coach and teacher to discuss issues that surface over time.
- Observations: Although many teachers will find being observed difficult, it is a great way for literacy coaches to learn about their teachers. You can observe the instructional methods that a teacher uses and suggest additional strategies that might enhance student learning.

Using an observation form can help focus your attention during an observation. You can use something as simple as the form in Figure 2.11, which focuses on a general reading lesson. As the teacher delivers each part of the lesson, you can record it on the form. If the teacher is not following the form's order, you can just add numbers to your notes to indicate the sequence of the lesson. Remember to keep all of these forms in your binder.

Depending on the situation you are observing, you may need to capture more than just the structure of the lesson—you may want to include information on classroom management and student-teacher interaction. When this is the case, you may want to use the form in Figure 2.12. The Tri-Perspective Ethnographic Observation Instrument (Medina, 2008) allows you to record your thoughts on the things that you see and hear during instruction. Linking your observational notes with something the teacher said or did will help you provide the teacher with concrete examples when discussing the lesson later. Figure 2.13 illustrates how this form can be used. It is an observation of the first 10 minutes of a guided reading lesson about immigration with a small group of students. The teacher then uses her notes from the lesson to inform her coaching conference.

Working With Groups: Professional Development Sessions

Along with working one-on-one with teachers, you will also be planning professional development sessions. These sessions can be small in scale and may be conducted during the hour set aside for a grade-level meeting, or they can be all-day events for the entire school staff during a teacher workday. The content will vary depending on your district and school needs. You can base your workshops on the needs survey conducted at the beginning of the year, on the principal's goals for reading growth, or on a predetermined curriculum mandated by the district or the grant that funds your position.

Regardless of the content of your session or of the size of the workshop, you should always prepare an agenda. The agenda will have several purposes. It will

- help keep your session focused
- provide the participants with an advanced organizer
- act as a way to document your time
- give you a place to take notes on the effectiveness of your session

These notes can later be used to make adjustments for the next time you do this session. Figure 2.14 gives you an example of a schedule that could be used for an all-day staff development. For a one-hour workshop, you may take just one of the elements from the all-day workshop agenda and expand on it for your shorter session.

Finally, you should also consider how you are going to collect feedback from your participants about the professional development session (see Chapter 6). Although it may be difficult to hear anything other than positive feedback after working hard to create an engaging workshop, it is an important step in the process. First, it sends a

Figure 2.11   General Observation Form

Teacher's Name _____   Date _____

Lesson Topic _____   Grade _____

Activation of prior knowledge:

Objective or purpose of lesson stated for students:

Teacher input (content of lesson):

Guided practice:

Independent practice:

Lesson closure:

Assessment:

Figure 2.12   Tri-Perspective Ethnographic Observation Instrument

What I Heard	What I Saw	What I Thought

Figure 2.13   Example of Completed Tri-Perspective Ethnographic Observation
                   Instrument

What I Heard	What I Saw	What I Thought
"Read me the word 'immigrant.' We read this word in one of our stories. Does anyone remember what it means?" Child reads answer from book.	Teacher sits at small table with three students.	What's the purpose of the lesson?
Teacher asks students where their parents are from. "Let's read about the immigrants who came to the United States a long time ago."	Rest of class seems to be working on something else; they are very loud.	Are the other students in the class actively engaged in learning?
Kids continue guided reading of text. Teacher asks questions about slaves based on the illustration.		Good use of visual to help clear up point. Would like to see kids read chorally or silently.
"Look at the map."	Teacher points to map.	Why aren't the rest of the kids participating in this lesson?
Students continue to take turns reading. Students in background shout, "WHAT? I can't believe you just said that to me!"		Have the other students been given a different assignment? Who's watching the rest of the class?
Teacher talks about groups forming a community. Gives example of Cuban community like the one the students are from and community in New York.		Glad you're making connections with prior knowledge. If you were a new parent or an office administrator walking into your class, what would you think? What would your impression be?

message to the participants that feedback is part of the growth
process for everyone. Second, it gives you the opportunity to read the
comments and adjust the workshop accordingly.

The feedback form you give to teachers can be very simple and
include only two questions:

- What aspects of this session did you find helpful?
- What aspects of this workshop would you change?

Or you can include more questions that focus on the literacy
content. For example:

- Are you planning to implement this literacy component in your
  classroom?

Figure 2.14 Sample Workshop Schedule

Reciprocal Teaching Workshop

9:00–10:00: Background and benefits of reciprocal teaching

10:00–10:30: Overview of four strategies

10:30–10:45: Break

10:45–11:15: Video and discussion of second graders using reciprocal teaching

11:15–12:00: Break into groups and do reciprocal teaching with article

12:00–1:00: Lunch

1:00–2:00: Implementing reciprocal teaching in your classroom

2:00–2:30: Meet with grade level and discuss implementation

2:30–3:00: Questions and comments

- What obstacles do you anticipate in implementing this literacy component?
- How can I support you in your implementation of this literacy component?

As a literacy coach, you will devote a great deal of your time to working with teachers on both individual and group levels. Your own reflection, as well as the feedback you receive from these interactions, can help you to build stronger and more engaging coaching sessions.

VOICES FROM THE FIELD

"You definitely have to be open-minded. You have to know that there is more than one way to do something. And you have to be accepting of teachers' personalities. You can't change their personalities."

Kelly

Wrapping Up the School Year

The end of the school year will bring about its own unique challenges. This section provides guidelines for inventorying material, closing the year's files, and preparing for the next school year.

The end of the year is always a time of reflection and reassessment. We need to look at our performance, the students' literacy growth, and teachers' progress critically. Were the expected gains made? If so, what aspects of literacy instruction are working? If the expected growth was not achieved, what can be done to ameliorate this for next year?

Two main projects will take up your time during these last days of school: inventorying material and closing the current year's files.

Inventorying Materials

If you are responsible for the school's supplemental reading program or professional development materials for teachers, you will probably spend some time at the end of the year doing inventory of what materials are still available, which materials need to be replaced, and what, if anything needs to be ordered. The first place to start is to inventory the current material. This is important because you need to make sure that all materials are returned and ready for the following school year. Figure 2.15 illustrates a sample inventory form that can be used to compile the information.

You may want to input this information into a software database. In this way, you can sort the information by reading level, potential grade level, or reading topic. This will help you to see quickly if there is a gap of reading material for a particular level, grade, or topic. If there are funds available, you may first want to replace any damaged or missing materials. Then, you may want to spend the rest of your money buying materials to fill any gaps you noticed.

Closing the Current Year's Files

Along with doing an inventory of materials, you need to reflect on the work you have done with teachers. Using your binders, revisit the work you have done with each teacher. Make sure everyone's file is complete. Make any necessary notations and remarks you feel necessary to summarize the progress you have made. Although the task may seem daunting at first, this is particularly important if you will be working with the same teachers next year. Having complete files

Figure 2.15 Sample Student Materials Inventory Form

Student Materials Inventory Form June 2008					
Title	Author	Publisher	Quantity	Potential Grade Level	Reading Level
Professional Resources Inventory Form June 2008					
Title	Author	Publisher	Quantity	Potential Grade Level	Reading Topic

and proper documentation will help you decide where to start when your coaching begins again.

This is also a good time to reflect on the workshops you have presented. Look through the agendas. Which workshops went well? Why do you think they were successful? Which sessions need improving? What can you do to make these sessions better? You can write down your thoughts on the agendas themselves, which will help you in your planning the following school year.

When you wrap up the school year, you evaluate and inventory materials, and then make remarks and annotations for yourself before closing your files. Take the time to reflect on those aspects of your coaching that were effective, as well as those that you would like to revise. Share your impressions with others to confirm their appropriateness and accuracy. Doing this can help you as you begin making plans for the next school year.

Next Steps: Professional Development Suggestions

1. Meet with other literacy coaches to discuss techniques for organizing and documenting the different aspects of your coaching roles. Then, implement at least one idea from this discussion that was new to you. At a follow-up meeting, evaluate how that technique worked and, if necessary, how it might be refined.

2. Collaborate with a group of literacy coaches to gather professional resources for different aspects of literacy learning. One or two coaches might gather resources for phonemic awareness; others might gather family literacy resources, and so on. Compile a comprehensive resource list based on the findings of individuals or teams so that all of the resources gathered can be used by all of the coaches.

3

The Heart of the Matter

Conferring With Teachers

In this chapter, we

- present a transcript of a teacher's lesson as a basis for framing supportive communication
- present observational notes written by a coach during the transcribed lesson to illustrate how coaches should take notes during observations
- present a transcript of a coaching conference to show how a literacy coach engages in a conversation with a teacher
- describe different phases of a coaching conference

When coaches confer with teachers, the real coaching begins. The bonds of rapport and trust are cemented as coaches and teachers come together and engage in meaningful conversations. These conversations are at the heart of coaching; professional knowledge is enriched when teacher and coach come together to discuss instructional practices.

During coaching conferences, coaches work with teachers to connect an ongoing literacy initiative with a current practice, engage teachers in genuine inquiry, and help teachers maintain a focus on student learning (Blachowicz, Obrochta, & Fogelberg, 2005). These conferences provide the literacy coach with an opportunity to establish a relationship of trust by listening carefully, maintaining confidentiality, and

---

VOICES FROM THE FIELD

"I wish I had known that my job was really about making teachers reflective about their own practice. At first I thought my job was about asserting my reflections on their instruction. I now realize that my reflection doesn't matter nearly as much as their reflections about their own teaching."

Elizabeth

---

following through with coaching commitments (Bean & DeFord, 2007). Effective coaching involves a collaborative dialogue with teachers that promotes a shared school vision about literacy, uses student data and teacher observations to drive instructional decisions, embeds professional engagement within the classroom, and encourages instructional discussions to develop over time (Shanklin, 2006). For meaningful change to take place within a school, the literacy coach needs time and space to confer with teachers (Neufeld & Roper, 2003). Table 3.1 outlines suggested phases for a teacher-coach conference.

A Teacher's Lesson

Carol Thomas is an early literacy coach who works with eight different teachers a week. Her teachers include one prekindergarten teacher, three kindergarten teachers, and four first grade teachers. She works with each teacher once a week, for a half day.

Ronda Smith, a kindergarten teacher, struggles with reading aloud books with her students. For the past few weeks, she has worried that her students were not interested in the texts and have not comprehended the texts read aloud. Last week, she asked Carol to observe her read-aloud instruction so they could discuss it.

When Ronda is ready to read a text aloud to the class, she gathers the students to the carpet and asks them to sit. They sit in a semicircle and face Ronda, who waits in a rocking chair. Carol sits behind the students and writes observational notes as she watches the lesson. Ronda begins:

Ronda: Today I'm going to read aloud a book. Our book is a big book. I like big books because I know everyone can see all the pages. The title of the book is *The Very Hungry Caterpillar* and the author is Eric Carle. Can someone tell me what an author does?

Table 3.1 Phases in a Coaching Conference

Phases of Conference	Coach's Role in the Conference	Teacher's Role in the Conference
Asking Questions	Ask a series of questions to gain more information: • initial questions • lesson questions • student-driven questions • connection questions • overarching questions	The teacher responds to the questions. The teacher offers reflective insights into what he or she did when teaching.
Explaining What the Coach Notices	State your observations: *These are some things that I noticed as you conducted this lesson. . . .* Continue to ask questions to deepen understanding.	Listen carefully to the coach's feedback. • Ask questions to clarify and deepen understanding. • Respond to feedback. • Continue to think reflectively about instructional practice.
Offering a Coaching Point	Offer one point about the lesson.	Listen to the coaching point and agree or disagree with the coach's advice. Decide if the coaching point is consistent with overall beliefs about teaching and learning.
Brainstorming Next Steps	Determine (with the teacher) next steps. Encourage the teacher to try out the next steps and report successes and challenges at the next conference.	Determine (with the coach) next steps. Have a go with the suggestions in the classroom.
Linking to Literature	Find and distribute practitioner and research articles and books concerning aspects of literacy. Read and discuss articles with the teacher.	Read articles and books provided by the coach. Engage in discussion with the coach about the readings.

Jimmy: The author writes the words.

Ronda: That's correct. The author writes all the words in the book. Eric Carle is also the illustrator of the book. Can someone tell me what the illustrator does?

Katie: He draws the pictures.

Ronda: Yes. The illustrator creates all the different pictures you see on the page. Some illustrators paint pictures, some draw using pencils, crayons, or chalk. And some make collages by gluing different pieces of paper together. Eric Carle illustrated this book by painting and making collages using different colored paper. That's something you could do today at the art center if you are interested.

Ronda: Okay, now I'm going to read the book. Turn on your listening ears. [Students pretend to turn up the volume on their ears.] Click on your thinking caps. [Students make clicking sounds on top of their head.] Let's read the book!

Ronda reads the book to the class, using inflection in her voice. The students listen as she reads each page. Occasionally, she runs her finger underneath the print to show the children that she reads the words on the page from left to right. After she reads the book, she asks a series of questions, and the students respond:

Ronda: What foods did that caterpillar eat?

Sarah: He ate apples.

Ronda: Yes. How many of those apples?

Sarah: Um . . . one apple.

Ronda: Let's look back in our book. [Ronda flips to the page.] That's right, he ate one apple. What other things did he eat?

Rodney: He ate cake.

Ronda: Yes he did. He ate a lot of sugary things. What other sugary things did he eat?

Ben: Lollipops.

Dottie: Ice cream.

Frank: Gum.

Ronda: Hmm . . . did the caterpillar eat gum? Let's go back in our book to find out. [She flips through each page.] Frank, do you see the caterpillar eating gum on any of the pages?

Frank: No.

Ronda: Well, that was a smart guess because he sure ate a lot of different things!

Frank: Yes. Like watermelon.

Ronda: That's right. Okay, that's the end of our book. Let's get ready for centers.

During Ronda's lesson, Carol wrote observational notes (see Figure 3.1). When possible, she transcribed the exact language Ronda and her students used when interacting. She did her best to capture the entire lesson, but paraphrased when needed. On the left side of her observational form, Carol recorded exactly what she saw. On the right side of the observational form, she recorded thoughts, things she noticed, and wonderings about the lesson. These notes will serve as her guide when she engages in the conversation with Ronda about the lesson.

Carol and Ronda find a time to confer when the students go to art. Before the meeting, Carol reads through her observational notes and decides how she will engage Ronda in genuine inquiry. Carol uses a flexible model to proceed with the conversation (see Table 3.2).

First, Carol will ask a series of probing questions to understand Ronda's instructional decisions. Carol, using her observational notes, will then explain what she noticed from the lesson. This sharing will lead to a discussion between Ronda and Carol; they will compare notes, ask follow-up questions, and determine the best way to proceed with future lessons. This culminates in a decision-making session. Together, Carol and Ronda will determine what Ronda needs to do next as a teacher and what Carol needs to do next as her coach. The transcribed conference below is broken into the different components of the conference session.

Asking Questions

Carol begins the first part of the lesson by asking Ronda a series of questions. During this initial part of the conference session, it is important for Ronda to think reflectively about her instructional practice before Carol interjects with what she noticed. Carol will proceed carefully throughout this part of the lesson to access Ronda's thoughts about the lesson.

Figure 3.1   Observational Notes Between Carol and Ronda

Teacher's Name: **Ronda Smith**   Date: **1-15-08**
Lesson Topic: **Reading Aloud — Comprehension of a Text**
Type of Observation:
☐ Coach Teaches Lesson/Teacher Observes: *I do, you watch.*
☐ Coach Teaches Lesson/Teacher Assists: *I do, You help.*
☑ Teacher Teaches Lesson/Coach Observes: *You do, I watch.*

Observations	Thoughts/Noticings/Wonderings
Ronda gathers student together on the carpet. R: Today I'm going to read aloud a book. Our book is a Big Book. I like them b/c everyone can see all the pages. The title is: *The Very Hungry Caterpillar*. The author is Eric Carle. What does the author do? Jimmy: Writes the words. R: Correct. The author writes all the words in the book. Carle is also the illustrator. What does the illustrator do? Katie: Draws the pictures. R: Yes. Creates all the different pictures you see on the page. Some paint pictures, use pencils, crayons, or chalk. Some make collages. Eric Carle made collages. That's something you could do today at the art center. R: Now, I'm going to read the book. Turn on your listening ears. Click on your thinking caps. Let's read the book. [Ronda reads the book. As she turns each page she occasionally runs her finger under the print. The students sit and face the book. Jenny and Rob start talking to one another during the story. Ronda keeps reading. She does not ask questions as she reads the story.] R: [After she has read the story, she asks questions] What does the caterpillar eat? Sarah: Apples R: Yes. How many? Sarah: Umm... one apple. R: Let's look back at our book. [flips to the page] Yes he ate one apple. What other things did he eat? Rodney: Cake R: Yes. He ate a lot of sugary things. What other sugary things? [Students shout out other answers. Frank said, "gum" which was not correct. Ronda looked back in the book to monitor answer.] Lesson ends. Ronda begins centers.	▸ Highlights Author / Title Why do you think it is important for students to know what the author/illustrator does? ▸ Explains all the different ways illustrators illustrate books. Why is this important? ▸ Connects with art center. ▸ Runs finger under print. Why is this important? Why on just a few occasions? ▸ Asks questions. What types of questions? Why questions only at the end of the read aloud? ▸ How do you handle students who answer questions incorrectly? ▸ How do you think the lesson ended?

Coach Action Steps: _____

_____

Teacher Action Steps: _____

_____

Carol: Okay . . . how do you think the lesson went?

Ronda: Well, it was better than it usually is. I think most of the students were paying attention. For the most part, they answered a lot of the questions correctly. So, I think most of them comprehended what the text was about.

Table 3.2   Types of Questions That Facilitate Genuine Inquiry in the Coaching Conference

Types of Questions	Examples
Initial Questions	• Overall, how do you think the lesson went? • Walk me through what you just did in this lesson. • What were you hoping to accomplish through this lesson?
Lesson Questions	• What did you do in the lesson to help students understand _____? • What was your goal when you did _____ during the lesson? • Why do you think it was important to teach this specific lesson?
Student-Driven Questions	• How do you think _____(student)_____ reacted to the lesson? • What did you notice about the students during the lesson? • How will you know if students understood the concepts you were trying to convey?
Connection Questions to Previous Discussions	• How have our previous discussions influenced this lesson? • Did any of our professional readings influence this lesson?
Overarching Questions	• How does this lesson fit into your overall beliefs about reading/writing? • How will this lesson help students as readers/writers?

Carol: Okay, so when you read aloud books to your class, what do you hope your students will learn?

Ronda: I want them to see a few different things. I want them to understand that I'm reading the print on the page. I want them to hear how reading sounds. I want them to stop and think about what they are reading and why they are reading this book.

Carol: So, what are you doing to help students understand that you are reading the print on the page?

Ronda: Well, I'm moving my finger under the print to show them the print-sound match. I'm using big books so they can actually see the words I am reading.

Carol: So, I noticed that you did that occasionally. You did not do that all the time. Why?

Ronda: Well, I don't think I need to put my finger under the words all the time. I also want them to know that some of the meaning is conveyed through the picture. So, I just do that sometimes.

Carol: You also said that you want them to hear how reading sounds. What do you mean by that?

Ronda: I want them to hear that when we read, we read with some inflection in our voices. That I just don't read with a monotone voice.

Carol: So why do you think that is important?

Ronda: I guess it goes back to the whole fluency thing. When we read aloud, we read in phrases; it's not choppy. I mean, I know most of these students are new readers, so of course they will read word by word. But I want them to hear how it sounds when a fluent reader is reading the words. I want them to fall in love with the melody of the words.

Carol: You also mentioned that you wanted the students to stop and think about what they are reading and why they are reading that book. Tell me how you did that in your read aloud today.

Ronda: Hmm . . . I asked questions at the end. But I'm not really sure I asked students to stop and think during the read aloud. I just read.

Carol: Do you think stopping them during the read aloud would have helped them think about what they are reading?

Ronda: Yeah. And I don't really think I do that enough. Hmm . . . maybe that is something I need to work on.

Carol: Last week you asked me to observe a read aloud because you worried that students were not engaged in the texts you read aloud. Do you think they were engaged in this one?

Ronda: Yes. They seemed like they really liked this book. Most of my students like Eric Carle. They were more excited about this book than other books I have read aloud.

Carol: Why do you think so?

Ronda: I think the illustrations are a big part of it. If the illustrations are good, the kids want to look at the book.

Carol: What types of books do you read aloud to the students?

Ronda: Well, mostly stories—books that have engaging illustrations. Mostly, I read the children's classics.

Carol: Are the read alouds mostly fiction?

Ronda: Yes. I would say they are mostly stories.

Carol: What do you think would happen if you used different genres to read aloud?

Ronda: Hmm . . . I'm not sure. Maybe I'll try that later today.

Explaining What the Coach Notices

Next, Carol shares with Ronda what she noticed during the lesson. Using her observational notes, Carol explains exactly what she saw during the lesson and continues to engage Ronda with genuine inquiry.

Carol: Okay. So now I'm going to go through my notes and tell you some things that I saw and we can talk about what you are thinking about.

Ronda: Sounds good.

Carol: First, I noticed that you highlighted the title and the author of the book. You asked students if they knew what authors and illustrators do. Jimmy explained that authors write words and Katie noted that the illustrator draws the pictures. You explained all the different ways that illustrators can illustrate books. Why do you think it was important for students to know what the author and illustrator do?

Ronda: Well, I actually ask those questions every time I read a book aloud. I guess I want them to know what an author does because I want them to see themselves as authors when they write books. I want them to know that when we write words on a piece of paper or in a book, we are assuming the role of writer. In terms of highlighting all the things an illustrator does, I want them to know that when they create illustrations for books, they have lots of choices in how to represent those illustrations. They don't have to use just markers. They can use crayons or pencils or cut paper or tissue paper. Illustrators use all sorts of materials to make their books.

Carol: You mentioned this before, but I think it is important that we talk about this a little further. I noticed that you ran your finger underneath some of the print on the pages. What was your purpose for that?

Ronda: Well, I just think it is important that my students know I'm actually reading some words on the page. I think at this age, naturally, the story is mostly told through the illustrations. But I wanted them to realize that the author wrote some words on there and when we read a book we have to attend to the words *and* the illustrations.

Carol: Yes. I agree. I think that is important. You are also showing them the routines readers go through to read books. They open books a certain way, they read from left to right, they stop when they see punctuation marks. You definitely modeled this in your teaching.

Ronda: Yes. Well, I think those things are important for kindergarten readers to learn.

Carol: Okay. So now I want to tell you some things I noticed about the questions you asked during the read aloud. You asked the students about the types of food the caterpillar ate, and the students answered the various questions. You asked things like, *What foods did the caterpillar eat? How many apples? What kinds of sugary things?* So, why did you choose to ask those specific questions?

Ronda: Well, I wanted to make sure they comprehended parts of the story. I wanted to see if they paid attention and understood what was read.

Carol: Do you think those specific questions helped you monitor their comprehension?

Ronda: Hmm . . . well, sort of. I think I showed them that they can always go back into the book to find answers to different questions. The text can help them do that.

Carol: I'm curious . . . how come you only asked questions at the end of the read aloud?

Ronda: I only asked questions at the end? I didn't ask any questions at the beginning or middle?

Carol: Well, you asked a couple questions about the author and illustrator at the beginning, but you saved the rest of the questions until the end.

Ronda: Yikes. Well, I think I probably should have stopped at a couple points during the story to monitor comprehension. I think I felt rushed because I wanted to make sure I got through the story before I lost their attention.

Offering a Coaching Point

VOICES FROM THE FIELD

"At first I was so evaluative. Big mistake! I really thought it was my job to go in there and tell teachers what they need to do to become better teachers. I was so wrong! I was even being evaluative when I didn't realize it. Like, I would say, 'That was one of your better lessons.' Or, 'That wasn't your strongest.' When I think about that, I want to cringe. That's not my job to make subjective statements about their lessons. I wish I had been more objective in my comments and less evaluative."

Kelly

Carol is now ready to offer Ronda a coaching point. During this phase of the conference, Carol will decide the one point she needs to make that will help push Ronda forward as a teacher. Carol could focus on many different issues surrounding the read-aloud session, but decides to tackle just one issue that she feels is the most pressing: modeling a process for comprehending texts.

Carol: Okay. So you mentioned that you should have stopped a couple of times while you read the story to monitor comprehension. Yes, I think that would help your students comprehend this specific story. However, I think it is important for young students to know how to monitor their comprehension as they read texts on their own. I think one thing you need to do when you conduct a read aloud is to explain to students the things you do as a reader that help you remember, understand, evaluate, and connect to a text. During read alouds, you model your reading process and give students a way that they can do the same when they read on their own.

Ronda: So, do you think I need to ask them a bunch of questions when I read a book aloud?

Carol: Well, I think it is important for you to show students how *they* could ask themselves questions when they are reading books on their own. Yes, I certainly think it is appropriate for you to monitor whether they comprehended *The Very Hungry Caterpillar* when you read the book aloud. But more importantly, I think you need to show them your process as a reader.

Ronda: Hmm . . . I haven't thought of it that way. Usually, when I read aloud, I just want them to comprehend the book I have read. I haven't really thought about why I do that. I guess it is not enough that they can just answer my questions. I want them to be able to do these things on their own.

Carol: I agree. But we have to keep in mind that they are kindergartners. In many ways, they are new to reading. You are doing so many things that are helpful for them as readers. You are showing them the print on the page, you are showing them left-to-right directionality, and you are showing them how to turn pages. Comprehension will come along with time. But read alouds are a great opportunity to show them what they can do as readers when they read a text.

Ronda: Yes. Okay, so I can start showing them how to read and comprehend texts by thinking out loud as I read aloud. This makes sense to me. So, this afternoon I'm reading aloud another book. Let's think of some things I should do when I read aloud.

Brainstorming Next Steps

At this point, Carol and Ronda are ready to discuss ways Ronda can show students her process in comprehending texts. They are ready to brainstorm next steps because Carol engaged Ronda in genuine inquiry, discussed and analyzed observational notes, and offered her a coaching point to support Ronda as a teacher. Together, they will decide what Ronda will do next in her classroom.

Carol: So when you read aloud your next book this afternoon, what are some things you are going to do?

Ronda: Well, I think I should react to the book the way I normally act on my own when I pick up a picture book for the first time. I am going to look at the cover, read the title, and look at who wrote the book to see if I recognize the name. Then I'm just going to flip through the book, look at the illustrations so I can get some sense of what this book is about. I'm not going to look at the end, though. As a reader, I like to be surprised at the end. I'm going to tell them that is what I do as a reader. After I do that, I'm going to start reading the book. I'll stop every few pages and remember some things about the story. I will do that throughout the read aloud.

Carol: I think that sounds like a good plan. I think you should also consider making some evaluative comments at the end of the read aloud. You may want to say out loud whether you liked the book or not. You may also think of a way you connect to the book. These are important things readers do when they read a text.

Ronda: Yes. I'm going to try that.

Linking to Literature

Finally, Carol is ready to connect Ronda to the literature. It is important that the teacher view the coach as a partner in the learning process, not the expert. Together, the coach and teacher read books and articles that support them as learners.

Carol: So my job this week is to find some articles that focus on reading aloud. I know of some research and practitioner-oriented articles we can read together that will push our thinking about this instructional practice. I'll find an article and put it in your mailbox in the next couple of days. When we meet next time, let's talk about what we read.

Ronda: Sounds like a plan!

Carol: Let's just take a minute and write this down so we don't forget.

In summary, Carol engaged Ronda in genuine inquiry during this coaching conference. She asked several questions to push Ronda's thinking and encouraged her to dissect the various components of the lesson. She ended the coaching session by finding a way to build Ronda's professional knowledge about reading aloud books to students. In the next section, we will look at how Carol structured this discussion.

Components of the Coaching Conference

A typical coaching conference lasts between 15 minutes and a half hour. During this time, the coach and the teacher engage in a conversation about a specific lesson with the intention of strengthening the professional knowledge of the teacher. The conference session progresses as a process that is composed of several parts: asking questions, noting observations, offering a coaching point, brainstorming next steps, and linking to the literature.

Asking Questions

During the first part of the conference, the coach inquires about the many instructional decisions a teacher makes in a lesson. Because these decisions occur consciously and subconsciously as the teacher instructs, it is important for the coach to break down the lesson by asking a series of questions. At this initial phase of the conference, the coach acts as information gatherer; asking questions to be an informed participant in the conversation. In this way, the coach engages teachers in reflective teaching. Different types of questions that can be asked during this phase of the conference are illustrated in Table 3.2.

Explain What the Coach Notices

After asking initial questions, the coach, sitting side by side with the teacher, provides an observational walk-through of the lesson.

During this phase of the conversation, the coach states what she saw during the lesson and asks specific questions about what she noticed. Taking detailed notes during the lesson becomes critical for the literacy coach; it provides an objective, data-driven narrative that the coach uses to deepen conversation.

The coach uses observational notes to make teachers aware of their instructional practices. When these become explicit to the teacher, the teacher can use these notes to reaffirm or change instructional beliefs and practices. This phase of the conversation allows the coach and teacher to objectively think about the lesson together; the coach probes further by asking more specific questions as the teacher engages in self-analysis.

The coach uses an observational form (see Figure 3.2) to record her observations of the lesson. Notice that this form is not a checklist; our goal as coaches is not to monitor teachers' ability to implement a packaged program and check off each component completed successfully. Rather, the observational form is used by the coach as a guide to engage the teacher in reflective inquiry. Checklists marginalize the complicated, intricate ways in which teachers engage their students in literacy acts. Some tips for taking observational notes include the following:

- Make a verbatim record of the teacher's lesson. As much as possible, write the *exact* words of the teacher and students.
- Use concrete details to describe what you see. For example, instead of *The student is happy*, you should write, *Dottie smiles as Ronda reads parts of the book. Dottie laughs each time the caterpillar eats through the different foods.*
- Avoid using language that judges or criticizes the teacher. For example: *Ronda doesn't do a good job asking questions: she only asks recall questions.* Instead, be specific. List the questions Ronda did ask and lead Ronda to discover the types of questions she asked during the conference.
- Do not write opinions about the effectiveness of the lesson on your observational notes.
- State what you see, not what you think.
- Write notes on duplicate paper or provide the teacher with a photocopy of your notes.

Offer a Coaching Point

After the coach and teacher have engaged in genuine inquiry and reviewed the observational notes of the lesson, the coach offers the

Figure 3.2   Observational Form

Teacher's Name: _____   Date: _____
Lesson Topic: _____
Type of Observation:
☐ Coach Teaches Lesson/Teacher Observes: *I do, you watch.* ☐ Coach Teaches Lesson/Teacher Assists: *I do, you help.* ☐ Teacher Teaches Lesson/Coach Observes: *You do, I watch.*

Observations	Thoughts/Observations/Wonderings

Coach Action Steps: _____

_____

_____

Teacher Action Steps: _____

_____

_____

_____

teacher input about the lesson. The purpose of this phase is for the coach to present her perspective and offer advice about one aspect of the lesson. This coaching point should be a suggestion, not a demand. And it comes after extensive inquiry with the teacher and teacher self-reflection. The language used during the coaching point phase of the conference is critical. Figure 3.3 offers suggestions of feedback pitfalls to avoid. Some tips for offering coaching points include the following:

- Focus on just one aspect of the lesson. It is important to maintain a clear focus when making this point. Offering more than one coaching point can overwhelm the teacher.
- Frame the coaching point within the school's overall beliefs about literacy.
- The coaching point should be offered in a nonthreatening manner. It is important for the teacher to feel that you are partners in this learning process.
- The coaching point should not take the majority of the time during the conference. Heavier time commitment should be given to the first two phases of the conference: asking questions and discussing the observation.
- Avoid using language that makes the teacher feel defensive. The coaching point should not make the teacher feel as if she has done something wrong.
- Make sure the coaching point is spoken in the spirit of maintaining rapport and building trust with the teacher. As the coach offers a point, she must keep in mind that her relationship with the teacher is a partnership. Coaching is not about teaching the teacher; it is about helping teachers teach themselves through reflective practice.

Brainstorm Next Steps

During the next phase, the literacy coach and teacher brainstorm next steps (see Figure 3.4). Together, they summarize what they learned from the conversation. Based on this discussion, the teacher considers how she can alter future lessons to accommodate new insights about her instructional practice. Brainstorming next steps is a critical phase of the coaching conference because it gives guidance for the teacher and a vision for what needs to happen next in the classroom.

This phase is not dictated by the coach. The coach works in conjunction with the teacher to decide what should happen next in the classroom. In turn, the teacher and the coach also decide next steps

Figure 3.3   Feedback Pitfalls to Avoid

Feedback Pitfalls to Avoid	
Type of Feedback Pitfall	*Example*
Making evaluative comments	*That was your best lesson yet.* *You didn't do a very good job on that lesson.*
Making judgments	*You are a terrific teacher.* *I can tell you really don't get along with that student.* *You don't seem very confident today in your teaching.*
Being overly critical	*I can't believe you would do something like that in your lesson!*
Getting off topic	*I know your lesson is about read alouds, but let's talk about your math instruction.* *What did you do this weekend?*
Offering solutions without teacher's input	*All you need to do is . . .* *This is what you need to do to fix your teaching. I'll be back next week to make sure you made those adjustments.*
Comparing teachers	*When I watched Kate do that lesson she did a better job of . . .* *You were much better than Charlie at that lesson.*
Engaging in school gossip	*Did you hear about . . .* *I know we need to talk about your lesson but can you believe . . .*
Proselytizing	*When I was a teacher this is what I did. . . . I think everyone should do the same.* *Listen, I know what I'm talking about. I've been a teacher for 20 years.*
Not using observations to guide instruction	*I think you did that during the lesson, but I'm not really sure.*

for the coach. Because they are partners in the classroom, each person assumes responsibility for promoting literacy in the classroom.

Linking to Literature

During the final phase, the coach links the teacher's instructional practices to practitioner-oriented articles and books. In this way, research and practice become a valued component of coaching conversations. Engagement and immersion with literature helps teachers realize there are other knowledgeable professionals who engage in instructional inquiries and have the fortitude to write about their experiences.

When teachers link with the literature, they connect with the greater literacy community. The authors of articles and books become distant mentors who guide teachers and deepen their professional knowledge. These mentors become the experts by helping teachers to push their thinking, consider alternatives, and support their beliefs. It is this prolonged engagement with professional literature that enriches the knowledge of teachers and guides their instructional decisions. Professional literacy organizations and their practitioner-oriented, peer-reviewed publications are in Table 3.3.

The bond between a coach and a teacher is critical for supporting reflective practitioners. When both people participate in rich conversations about instructional practice, learning occurs. The coach fosters this relationship by conducting coaching conferences that encourage, support, and help teachers engage in genuine inquiry and self-reflection. Teachers benefit from these conversations because the coach helps to deepen thinking and offer perspective. Ultimately, students are enriched because their teachers develop ways to enhance their learning.

Figure 3.4   Illustration of Action Steps Recorded on the Observational Form

Coach Action Steps: Find Read Aloud articles from The Reading Teacher and Young Children. Read articles and discuss with Ronda next week.
Teacher Action Steps: ①During next read aloud, model the process you use as a reader; ②Ask questions before, during, and after read aloud; ③Read a couple Read Aloud articles.

Table 3.3   Literacy Organizations and Their Practitioner-Oriented, Peer-Reviewed Publications

Professional Literacy Organization	Practitioner-Oriented, Peer-Reviewed Publications
Association for Childhood Education International www.acei.org	Childhood Education
International Reading Association www.reading.org	The Reading Teacher Reading Online
National Association for the Education of Young Children www.naeyc.org	Young Children Beyond the Journal
National Council of Teachers of English www.ncte.org	Language Arts School Talk Talking Points Classroom Notes

Next Steps: Professional Development Suggestions

1. Role-play a coaching conference with another literacy coach. Discuss a challenge you currently have with a teacher and practice the conversation with another coach. Include the following phases of the conference in your role-play:

   - asking questions
   - explaining what you notice
   - offering a coaching point
   - brainstorming next steps
   - linking to the literature

2. Use a video recorder to record the teacher's lesson. Video recording will allow the teacher to see the lesson from an outsider's perspective. Instead of using the observational notes to explain what you notice, pause the recorded lesson and discuss what you both see at specific intervals.

4

Assessment

Using Data to Inform Literacy Instruction

(with Stephen Hancock)

In this chapter, we

- explain how literacy assessment data can be used to improve literacy instruction
- describe different types of literacy assessment
- offer practical scenarios to help teachers make authentic connections between assessment and instruction

On virtually every public school district Web site, assessment data are only two clicks away. The assessments cover everything from reading and writing to science and mathematics. While the tests give the public a snapshot of how students *might* be doing in schools, the data do not suggest practical strategies that will enable teachers to improve student learning. In fact, many of the data are not meant to inform instruction, but are designed instead to present a broad brushstroke of student achievement (Kohn, 1999). Different constituencies need different types of information, presented in different forms, and made available at different times (Farr, 1992). While district level administrators, for example, need data about student progress across

---

VOICES FROM THE FIELD

"No matter what, the students guide your coaching conversations. You talk with teachers based on what you notice about the literacy habits of the students. When I coach, I ask the teacher, 'What do you notice about your students? How did they react to the lesson?' The students provide the foundation for the types of discussions you have with teachers."

Ben

---

grade levels and schools, teachers need data that illuminate individual students' literacy learning progress. Teachers also need to understand the relationship between testing and teaching.

For many early childhood and elementary programs, acquiring literacy concepts is the hallmark of learning and student success. Effective teaching is marked by an ability to use assessments as an integral part of teaching and learning. Teachers of young children need instruction, practical support, and modeling to improve their ability to effectively teach literacy concepts.

Unfortunately, many teachers are unaware of the benefits, strategies, and methods to improve student literacy through the use of assessment data. Fox (2004) contends that, all too often, teachers see little connection between assessment data and the potential to use those data to improve instructional practices and, in turn, student achievement. Literacy coaches can help teachers to bridge the gap between assessment and instruction. Teachers who lack the ability to make sound instructional decisions based on assessment data may lose important opportunities to improve students' literacy development.

In addition, the growing pressure for early childhood educators to produce kindergartners who are ready to read mounts higher every day, and in urban schools the stakes are even higher. Hence, it is critical for teachers to understand how assessment data can better inform and improve instruction in literacy development. Toll (2005) contends that a teacher-centered approach to understanding teaching, learning, and assessment is the responsibility of literacy coaches. A literacy coach is different from a reading specialist in that coaches are focused on fulfilling the professional needs of the teacher as well as modeling learning strategies for students. A teacher-centered approach to improving instruction, then, also requires a coach to help educators understand how assessments relate to teaching and learning. Toll (2005) describes literacy coaches as a

- support for teachers' professional and instructional needs and concerns
- model and teacher for students
- support for instructional decisions based on student evaluations
- one-on-one or small-group guide to lead teachers through instructional and assessment dilemmas

Literacy coaches are needed to provide teachers with a realistic and practical outlook on using assessment data to improve literacy instruction.

A Child-Centered Perspective of Assessment

Child-centered analysis of assessment data implies that a student's academic strengths are taken into account as the teacher evaluates progress and challenges. Assessment for young children should not be a separate part of instruction. In fact, each time a child reads, speaks, writes, acts, draws, builds, plays, or displays any learning concept can be viewed as a potentially assessable moment—a moment in which teachers obtain information about a child's understanding of literacy concepts. Literacy coaches can play an important role in guiding teachers toward understanding that assessment data should be analyzed from a student-centered perspective. By doing so, teachers can better select instructional strategies that are geared to the needs and development levels of each student (Jonston & Lawrence, 2004). For example, if a student has challenges with reading comprehension but is proficient in vocabulary development, a child-centered approach to analyzing test results will guide a teacher toward instructional strategies for strengthening comprehension through the use of vocabulary strategies.

Literacy coaches can also assist teachers in understanding the types of literacy assessments as well as how to select appropriate assessments and apply assessment results to instructional planning. In fact, tests become useless and meaningless if they don't positively impact and inform instructional practices. Literacy coaches need to convey the message that effective assessments should evaluate what is being taught, provide a pathway for instruction, and measure student achievement.

It is the responsibility of the literacy coach to inform teachers that the nexus of student achievement lies in a teachers' ability to effectively observe academic progress and to develop relevant and effective lessons that respond to student needs. Being able to choose, administer, and analyze appropriate assessments for children are practices that teachers must adopt to effectively use tests to inform teaching. Many teachers require assistance and support in transferring test results to instructional strategies. In fact, Neuman, Copple, and Bredekamp (2001) contend that assessment should be at the heart of instruction. The process of recording, documenting, and observing what children do and how they engage in literacy experiences should be the fundamental component in choosing and administering assessments as well as in planning instructional practices. Thus, it is important for the literacy coach to support teachers in their efforts to implement the following five principles of effective assessment practices (Neuman et al., 2001):

1. Monitor and document children's progress over time.

   Good literacy assessments are ongoing and they provide helpful information that informs the teacher about the progress of students. Literacy evaluations can take place whenever a child speaks, writes, reads, draws, or pretends. For example, when a child engages in pretend play, the teacher may observe by watching the child's play episode that the child understands story sequence. As a result, the teacher may ask the child to talk about his or her pretend episode and assess whether it has a beginning, middle, and end.

2. Ensure that instruction is culturally responsive and developmentally appropriate.

   The result of every literacy assessment tool should be to inform instruction. To that end, the instruction must be culturally relevant and developmentally appropriate. For instance, if the literacy assessment shows that a child does not recognize beginning sounds, instruction that uses words and pictures that are developmentally appropriate but also socially and culturally familiar to the student may help to ensure a greater margin of success.

3. Tailor instruction to enhance learning strengths and build up weaknesses.

   The data received from literacy assessment should inform teachers of strengths and challenges a child may possess. As a result, teaching strategies and methods should be customized to meet the needs of the student. Examples of such assessment tools are discussed later in this chapter.

4. Provide children with an opportunity to observe their own successes and challenges.

Effective literacy assessments can be presented in a way that enables young children to begin to monitor their own learning progress and become aware of their improvements as literacy learners. For example, teachers can create simple charts to summarize growth, or they can provide authentic portfolios that show students how their work has progressed over time.

5. Guide intensive remediation or advanced instruction for children.

Literacy assessment can guide teachers toward remediation activities or toward more challenging activities. For example, if a weakness in a literacy concept is revealed as a result of an assessment, the teacher should be able to provide intensive and appropriate remediation for the student in an effort to increase the student's understanding of the concept.

Assessments should be an integral part of everyday instruction. When assessments are student centered, teachers are better able to pinpoint learning gaps and strengths (Jonston & Lawrence, 2004). The information derived from such assessments can help teachers to create lessons and learning opportunities appropriate to meet individual learning needs. Table 4.1 is a checklist to guide literacy coaches in their efforts to assist teachers in using assessment results to inform instructional practices.

Types and Forms of Literacy Assessment for Early Readers

It is imperative that literacy coaches transfer information about assessment to teachers through workshops and mentoring conversation. Information about the different types of assessments available to them may be helpful information for classroom teachers. Literacy assessments can be categorized into two broad assessment types: *formal assessments* and *informal assessments*. Formal assessments are often produced by testing agencies or entities outside of the school. They are typically administered under standardized conditions and are intended to provide information about student performance at a specific point in time (Walker, 2008). Formal assessment data are often used to compare peers within a representative group of students. The test results from these assessments are normally scored to produce a

Table 4.1   Assessment and Instruction Checklist

Item	Yes	No
1. Assessment influences instruction.		
2. Assessment measures what was taught.		
3. Appropriate assessment is administered.		
4. Assessment is analyzed from a student-centered perspective.		
5. Assessment and instruction are used to monitor progress over time.		
6. Assessment and instruction are culturally appropriate.		
7. Instructional practices address strengths and weaknesses.		
8. Assessment is used to guide remediation and advanced instruction.		
9. Assessment provides students opportunities to see challenges and success.		
10. Assessment and instruction are developmentally appropriate.		

standardized outcome and can be easily used by a state, region, school district, or single class. With the exception of chapter tests from textbooks, professionally made tests usually are equipped with rules on how to score and analyze the results. Unfortunately, these tests may not be sensitive to learning or cultural differences in young children. As increased emphasis has been placed on accountability in schools, formal assessments have been used with greater frequency to measure student achievement and the overall effectiveness of schools and districts (Mraz & Kissel, 2007).

By contrast, informal assessments are often created by teachers and are usually idiosyncratic to particular students and classrooms. Informal assessments are intended to collect information about what students do as they engage in the process of reading and writing. Informal assessments that are teacher-made assessments are created by the teacher, administrator, or faculty body and are specific to the school, classroom, or student. Teacher-made assessments tend to be more personal, relevant, and practical for teachers and students. Teacher-made assessments are important assessment tools because they are typically authentic representations of what has been taught, sensitive to the developmental needs of children, and can be created to attend to cultural differences in learning and testing styles.

Informal assessments may involve tools such as miscue analyses and running records. They may also include anecdotal observations made by the teacher while a child engages in reading or writing, samples of student work, teacher-student conferences, attitude and interest surveys, and checklists of developmental behaviors and skills (Morrow, 2005). Literacy coaches need to understand the fundamental difference between formal assessments and informal assessments. They must also understand how each assessment form can be used to effectively support literacy instruction and learning.

Professional Assessments for Literacy

Regardless of the form, literacy assessments for young children aged three to five years should support their knowledge of phoneme identity, letter knowledge, rhyme recognition, knowledge about print, and receptive and expressive vocabulary (Hindson et al., 2005). For elementary school children aged six to eight years, literacy assessments often focus on reading comprehension, reading fluency, grammar, punctuation, and vocabulary development. Below are descriptions of sample professional assessment tools commonly used in early literacy instructions for phoneme identity, letter recognition, receptive vocabulary, reading fluency, and comprehension and their teacher-made counterparts.

- Phoneme identity

  Description: This 20-item assessment is designed to evaluate a student's ability to hear and match the beginning sounds of familiar objects. The assessment measures phonemic awareness, initial sound differentiation, and simple sound decoding (Byrne & Fielding-Barnsley, 1991).

  Material: Test booklet

  Procedure: Using pictures and oral communication, children are asked to select a word or picture that has the same beginning sound of a target picture or word (Hindson et al., 2005).

  Time: 15–20 minutes per student

- Letter recognition

  Description: This assessment is designed to evaluate children's visual knowledge of letters. The results of this test provide information about letter knowledge and possible name-sound relationships (Byrne & Fielding-Barnsley, 1991).

Material: Test booklet

Procedure: This letter knowledge assessment is a multiple-choice test that asks children to select one lowercase letter from a group of four letters to match a verbal letter name spoken by the examiner (Hindson et al., 2005).

Time: 10–15 minutes

- Early literacy development

Description: Dynamic Indicators of Basic Early Literacy Skills (DIBELS) assessments are commonly used standardized measures of early literacy development that can be used to monitor students' early reading skills in kindergarten through sixth grade. These measurements can help to assess students' knowledge of initial sounds, letter naming, phoneme segmentation, oral reading, retelling, and word use. Similarly, Individual Growth and Development Indicators (IGDIs) are designed to be used with preschoolers to help monitor early reading development tasks including alliteration, rhyming, picture naming, and letter naming.

Material: Standardized DIBELS or IGDI materials, which vary according to grade levels

Procedure: Test administrator follows the standardized procedures for administering the DIBELS or IGDI assessments.

Time: DIBELS uses a series of one-minute fluency measures. IGDIs are designed to estimate a child's growth over time and can be used repeatedly to do so. The time required for the administration of IGDIs varies according to each child's level of literacy development.

- Receptive vocabulary

Description: Receptive vocabulary of young children can be measured by the Peabody Picture Vocabulary Test-Revised (PPVT-R). Dunn and Dunn (1981) created Forms L and M to assess children's accessible vocabulary or words students have experienced (Hindson et al., 2005). This assessment can provide information about reading potential, beginning comprehension, and word knowledge.

Material: Form L or Form M; picture vocabulary book

Procedure: The test administrator places the picture vocabulary book in front of student. The test administrator uses Form L or

Form M to score students and proceeds to read each vocabulary word aloud. The test administrator marks on the form the incorrect response and repeats the word while pointing to the correct response. The student continues until 8 out of 10 consecutive responses are incorrect.

Time: Open-ended; assessments can be as short as 5 minutes and as long as 45 minutes.

- Reading fluency and comprehension

  Description: The Directed Reading Assessment (DRA) is designed to evaluate oral reading components such as phrasing and intonation, and reading strategies such as rereading, picture clues, and decoding (Beaver, 1999). The DRA also evaluates reading comprehension through the use of retelling and both convergent and divergent questions.

  Material: DRA observation guide; leveled book; typed copy of the story

  Procedure: The test administrator provides the student with a leveled book and encourages the student to read. The test administrator uses a typed copy of the story to record miscues as the student reads. The test administrator also monitors reading using the observation guide. At the conclusion of reading, the test administrator presents the student with comprehension questions. Results are recorded on an observational guide (Beaver, 1999).

  Time: 5–15 minutes

Teacher-Made Assessments for Literacy

Unlike professional assessments, which are developed by publishers or professional assessment organizations, teacher-made assessments are developed by teachers for the purpose of assessing particular aspects of students' literacy development within the authentic and informal setting of the classroom. Explained below are examples of teacher-made assessments that can be administered using materials commonly found in classrooms.

- Beginning sound

  Description: This assessment is designed to evaluate a student's ability to hear and match the beginning sounds of familiar objects. The assessment measures phonemic awareness, initial sound differentiation, and simple decoding by sound.

Material: Five focus items (normally shapes, toys, or pictures) all with a different beginning sound. For example, the focus items could be a *b*ook, *w*ell, *c*oat, *h*at, and *a*pple. The teacher should also provide eight items for matching; five of the eight items should have the same beginning sound as the focus items. For example, the items for matching could include a *b*oat, *w*eed, *c*at, *h*orse, *a*nt, pear, sail, and tape.

Procedure: The teacher places one focus item at the top of the row and four of the eight matching objects in a row beneath the focus item. After naming both the focus item and matching items, the teacher asks the child to match the item that has the same beginning sound as the focus item. If the child is correct, he or she gets to keep both the focus item and the matching items. If the child is incorrect, the teacher models how to find the correct answer and takes the two items with the same beginning sound. The teacher replaces one matching item and provides a new focus item. There should always be four matching items and one focus item. The teacher should always be sure that there is an object that has the same sound as the focus item.

Time: 5–10 minutes

- Letter knowledge

  Description: This assessment is designed to evaluate children's visual knowledge of letters. The results of this test provide information about letter knowledge and letter name-sound relationships.

  Material: Magnetic letters (uppercase and/or lowercase); magnetic board

  Procedure: The teacher chooses letters that are both easy and challenging for the student. Using the magnetic board, the teacher places a maximum of 10 letters on the board; the number of letters used may vary depending on the developmental level of the child. The teacher encourages the child to pick the letter spoken by the teacher. If the child chooses the correct letter, he or she may take the letter. If the child picks an incorrect letter, the teacher models and shows the child the correct letter by saying the letter name and removing the letter from the board.

  Time: 5–10 minutes

- Vocabulary challenge

  Description: This assessment is designed to evaluate a student's accessible vocabulary, or words the student has experienced.

This test can provide information about reading potential, beginning comprehension, and word knowledge.

Material: 20 picture cards (flash cards)

Procedure: The teacher selects 20 picture cards (flash cards) with a variety of concepts (e.g., vehicles, emotions, actions/activities, objects, animals, plants, insects). The teacher places four pictures in front of the child and asks the child to pick the picture spoken by the teacher. If the child selects the correct picture, the picture is given to the child. If the child selects an incorrect picture, the child is shown the correct picture and the teacher removes the picture and replaces it with a new picture. The teacher repeats this process, leaving three pictures and replacing one.

Time: 10–15 minutes

- Reading and comprehension

  Description: This teacher-made assessment is designed to evaluate student reading fluency and comprehension through a series of questions and reading strategies.

  Material: A picture book that is unfamiliar to the student and is preferably leveled or reasonably challenging; paper and pencil; five comprehension questions, both literal and interpretive, that are associated with the story

  Procedure: The teacher encourages the student to read the story aloud and writes down any words that are challenging for the student to pronounce, as well as words that the student does not understand. The teacher models the correct pronunciation and provides contextual meanings for unknown words. The student rereads the story once. Then, the teacher asks the student the comprehension questions.

  Time: 10–20 minutes

It is important to note that both formal and informal assessments are important in developing proficient literacy learners. While formal assessments can provide data that look at overall progress, these assessments can also provide information about how individual students are functioning in comparison with their peers at similar developmental levels. In addition, formal assessments afford educators an opportunity to look at literacy issues across age groups and learning stratifications. By contrast, informal assessments can offer a more specific comparative analysis among students within individual classrooms. For example, teachers can analyze the degree to which certain instructional strategies have helped students to achieve literacy learning objectives. The use of both types of assessment is important for developing appropriate instruction and interventions to foster proficient literacy development.

Using Assessment Data to Inform Instruction

Literacy coaches need to convey to teachers the importance of using both professional and teacher-made assessment data to inform literacy instruction. Thus, it is imperative that teachers embrace four basic principles for connecting tests to teaching. First, educators must have a clear reason for choosing the assessment instrument. Second, to create effective instructional opportunities for students, educators must clearly understand the concepts and skills that are being assessed. Third, educators should know what the assessment intends to measure and how it will be scored. Finally, teachers must recognize how the assessment data can guide instruction. Key aspects of each principle are described below.

- Why this assessment

  Teachers should pose four basic questions before formally evaluating any student:

  1. What information or instructional knowledge am I looking to gain from the assessment?
  2. What concept or skill is being assessed?
  3. Does assessment genuinely and authentically evaluate the target concept or skill?
  4. Are the assessment results representative of the child's progress as reflected by other formal and informal assessment measures?

- Understand the concept or skill being tested

  It is important for educators to understand the concept or skill that is being assessed. For example, when children are given the PPVT-R, test administrators should recognize that the test assesses receptive and visual vocabulary; the PPVT-R evaluates a child's readily accessible vocabulary through the use of pictures and verbal cues. However, the test is limited to those words that are used in the evaluation and may not exhaust a child's total vocabulary. Additionally, the test is based on mainstream words and, in many instances, may not reflect cultural meanings and idiosyncrasies. For example, if the word spoken in the test administrator is *pail* and the child knows the picture of the pail as a *bucket*, then the child may not choose the correct picture for *pail*. Nonetheless, it is imperative that teachers are aware of what receptive vocabulary means and how it can impact children's reading, writing, listening, and speaking.

- Know what the assessment intends to measure and how it will be scored

  Teachers need to understand how to interpret scores and evaluative outcomes. For example, what does it mean if a four-year-old earns a 4–5 age equivalent on the PPVT-R? According to the PPVT-R, the score means that a child has a high-average vocabulary. Teachers, then, should understand that the assessment will measure vocabulary by age-equivalent outcomes.

- Analyze the connection between assessment and instruction

  Analyzing assessment data to inform instruction is one of the most important factors in successful teaching. For example, if the teacher learns that a four-year-old student has earned a 4–5 age equivalent on the PPVT-R, the assessment result reveals that the child has a high-average vocabulary. The teacher then must prepare to further support and expand the child's vocabulary. To ensure further growth, the teacher can provide the child with stimulating instruction. Activities may include "sophisticated talk," an intentional use of vocabulary by teacher that requires the child to ask for word meanings and eventually incorporate the use of those words into the child's own speech; concept sort, using picture cards with words to categorize in topics; and reading unfamiliar picture books that stretch vocabulary through words and pictures. Increased word knowledge and usage will likely lead to stronger reading skills, increased vocabulary, and writing proficiency.

While most professional assessments provide a process for measuring student performance, it is important that teacher-made tests are equipped with a systematic and relevant process for evaluating children's performance. Literacy coaches should suggest to teachers that it is good practice to use more than one assessment tool to evaluate a skill or concept. Though the tests may assess the same concept, multiple evaluative tools that focus on specific skills create a stronger and more reliable picture of student knowledge. In supporting teachers in their efforts to link assessment data to their instructional practices, Table 4.2 provides examples of the ways in which professional and teacher-made assessments can be correlated to specific skill challenges and instructional strategies.

To create classrooms where literacy instruction is effective, coaches must guide teachers toward using assessment tools as integral parts of instruction. Literacy coaches should reiterate the concepts that assessments should not be viewed as unconnected bits of information that stand apart from lesson plans and learning strategies. Rather, assessments should drive how learning is directed and constructed in the classroom.

Table 4.2   Early Literacy Skills Assessments and Instructional Strategies

Skill	*Professional Assessment*	*Teacher-Made Assessment*	*Instructional Strategy*
Receptive Vocabulary	Peabody Picture Vocabulary Test	Vocabulary Challenge	Concept sorts, sophisticated talk, word games, songs, rhyming games, listening to and reading a variety of literature
Comprehension	Directed Reading Assessment	Reading/ Comprehension	Story-retell activities, word-decoding strategies, listening to and reading a variety of literature, story sequencing, read alouds, shared reading, reading centers
Letter Recognition	Letter Knowledge	Letter Names and Sounds	Songs, artistic expressions, letter name games, puzzles, and letter-writing activities
Initial Consonant	Phoneme Assessment	Beginning Sounds Test	Beginning sound word sort games, tongue twisters, alliteration poems, beginning sound picture sort games

Practical Vignettes

The following scenarios are prepared for literacy coaches to assist them as they lead teachers in applying steps to connect assessments to instruction. These vignettes can be used as part of ongoing professional development sessions that are intended to enhance teachers' professional knowledge of the connections between assessment and instruction. Potential responses are offered for each vignette; however, literacy coaches should encourage teachers to elaborate on their own responses and consider the unique learning needs among their own students.

Vignette 1

Eight-year-old Lamar is an energetic and talkative child. He thrives on interactions with peers, adults, and books. He especially likes reading and talking about his favorite stories and topics. Lamar has done well on teacher-made evaluations of his vocabulary, reading fluency, and comprehension. He has mastered many sight words and can read familiar text by using picture cues to call out words. When introduced to an unfamiliar book, Lamar's difficulty with decoding unfamiliar words interferes with his comprehension of the text. The teacher is uncertain of what to do to enhance Lamar's reading skills.

Literacy Coach Recommendations

1. Based on previous instructional activities and observations, articulate the reasons why Lamar needs to be assessed.

   Coach's recommendation: Lamar should be tested because of his inability to read unfamiliar text. He relies heavily on memory and "easily" decodable words; however, he is unable to transfer this knowledge to new reading experiences.

2. Decide on what skill or concept will be assessed.

   Coach's recommendation: Lamar's decoding skills and vocabulary development should be assessed.

3. Choose assessments and understand how they will measure performance.

   Coach's recommendation: The PPVT-R or a teacher-made vocabulary test should be administered to evaluate Lamar's vocabulary level. The PPVT-R will help the teacher pinpoint Lamar's age-equivalent vocabulary. Lamar should also receive a DRA to evaluate his challenges in decoding words and reading fluency.

4. Connect results to instructional activities that will enhance student progress.

   Coach's recommendation: The teacher should engage Lamar in listening to and reading a variety of literature. Lamar should be encouraged to use higher vocabulary words in conversation and create written narratives from his favorite stories. Verbal word games, decoding activities, and phonemic awareness experiences may also be beneficial.

Vignette 2

Lisa is six years old and loves to sing. She is active during recess and loves pretending and creating works of art. Her favorite activity is sorting and/or matching any set of objects. Lisa knows sight words and environmental words; however, she is unable to pronounce middle vowel sounds in unfamiliar words. For example, she had difficulty reading the words "pout" and "ceiling." What should Lisa's teacher do?

Literacy Coach Recommendations

1. Based on previous instructional activities and observations, articulate the reasons why Lisa needs to be assessed.

   Coach's recommendation: Lisa should be tested because she is having difficulty recognizing middle vowel sounds.

2. Decide on what skill or concept will be assessed.

   Coach's recommendation: Lisa's vowel sound recognition should be assessed, as well as her knowledge of vowel patterns.

3. Choose assessments and understand how they will measure performance.

   Response: A phoneme assessment that concentrates on vowel sounds should be administered. A PPVT-R will help determine Lisa's vocabulary level and assist in choosing appropriate words for her phoneme assessment.

4. Connect results to instructional activities that will enhance student progress.

   Coach's recommendation: The teacher should engage Lisa in phonemic activities that explore vowel sounds. Instruction should be modified so that Lisa is able to sort and match vowel sounds in common categories. In addition, phonetic patterns of regular vowel sounds should be introduced.

Vignette 3

Jonathan is four years old. He loves to build, run, play, and paint. He is attentive when he is able to move his body, and he enjoys field trips and outings. He enjoys listening to familiar stories but is not able to sit more than 7–10 minutes. He can sing the alphabet song and he recognizes his own name. Jonathan knows the names of the letters in his name but is unfamiliar with most of the other letters. While he is showing promising signs of letter-sound knowledge, Jonathan is able to recognize many letters. What should Jonathan's teacher do?

Literacy Coach Recommendations

1. Based on previous instructional activities and observations, articulate the reasons why Jonathan needs to be assessed.

   Coach's recommendation: Jonathan should be tested because he is not able to recognize all the letters by name.

2. Decide what skill or concept will be assessed.

   Coach's recommendation: Letter recognition will be assessed.

3. Choose assessments and understand how they will measure performance.

   Coach's recommendation: The letter knowledge test or the letter name and sound test should be administered.

4. Connect results to instructional activities that will enhance student progress.

   Coach's recommendation: The results of Jonathan's assessment may indicate that he would benefit from the use of strategies such as alphabet puzzles, letter matching activities, songs, and letter name games.

As literacy coaches attempt to provide teachers with practical solutions for using assessments in the classroom, it is important to maintain a professional yet sensitive perspective on the teacher's knowledge, abilities, and experiences. Therefore, coaches should consider the 10 tips listed in Table 4.3 as they assist in helping teachers connect assessment to instruction.

Coaches are responsible for assisting teachers in the analysis of assessment results, preparing proper environments for testing, and being sure that the assessment matches the needs of the student. As models for teachers, coaches should also support teachers by providing practical strategies that help connect assessment to instruction.

Table 4.3   Ten Assessment and Instruction Tips for Coaches

When using assessment to inform instruction, coaches should

1. help teachers understand the difference between and the importance of informal assessments as well as formal assessments.

2. develop teachers' knowledge of how to analyze and score assessments.

3. assist teachers in preparing appropriate assessment conditions.

4. ensure that concepts or skills are being evaluated with appropriate assessment tools.

5. help teachers understand strategies to effectively connect assessment outcomes to instructional strategies.

6. help teachers understand that stronger student academic profiles are developed when a variety of assessment forms are used to evaluate the same skill.

7. assist teachers in understanding the content and purpose of formal assessment material and instructions.

8. provide support and practical assistance to effectively teach teachers how to create their own teacher-made, informal assessment tools.

9. help teachers develop clear goals and expectations for linking assessment to literacy instruction.

10. encourage teachers to assess skills frequently to support their instruction.

Next Steps: Professional Development Suggestions

1. Develop and implement an informal workshop for teachers at which you display and demonstrate the use of different formal and informal assessment tools. Invite teachers to share other assessment tools that they find to be useful when working with students.

2. Working with other literacy coaches, analyze assessment data samples and discuss the recommendations that you might make to teachers based on these data.

3. Working with a teacher study group, conduct individual case studies of students. Ask teachers to collect observational notes, assessment data, and writing samples of a specific student or students in their class. Together, as a study group, encourage the teachers to identify ways to modify instruction to meet the students' individual needs.

5

Learning Communities

Supporting Collaborative Teamwork

In this chapter, we

- define a school learning community
- describe different types of school learning communities
- state purposes for each school learning community
- explain how coaches can foster productive communities within the school

A first-year teacher staples letters to her bulletin board to create her first word wall. A veteran teacher arranges desks for her 20th time. A vice principal, new to the school, works on the lunch schedule for the year. A mother buys school supplies for her daughter who anxiously waits to hear who her third grade teacher will be. All are members of a school community. With the help of a literacy coach, they can merge to become members of an effective learning community.

All teachers know the isolation of the classroom and become accustomed to the silence. Apart from the occasional observation of the principal or visit from a parent volunteer, the majority of instructional time takes place between teacher and students, with almost no opportunity to interact socially with peers or other school participants.

When teachers lack the opportunity to network with peers, schools become limited learning organizations (Lashway, 1997). Instead, schools need to be vibrant places where participants engage in reflective dialogue, focus on student learning, continuously interact, and collaborate around a shared vision of learning (Louis & Kruse, 1995). Schools need to be places where all those involved in the education of children become part of a greater learning community.

VOICES FROM THE FIELD

"This job is 20% content knowledge and 80% personality. Obviously, it is so important that you have a great deal of knowledge about literacy and experience teaching literacy processes to young children. However, so much of this job is working with people in a way that builds them up and strengthens their instruction. To do this, you have to establish a real trusting relationship. The teachers you work with really have to like and respect you for you to make any kind of difference in their classrooms. If you have an abrasive or confrontational personality, you will not do well in this job."

Ben

School Learning Communities

School learning communities are teams of people who share and develop knowledge, construct consensus, engage in periodic reviews of achievements or challenges, and work together to improve the overall learning of students (DuFour, 2003). When these teams come together, they reflect on teaching and learning, work toward a shared vision for the school, and build collegiality among school participants (Marzano, 2003). The coach works to facilitate this collective learning by working with various participants who play significant roles in the development of student learning. The community participants (see Figure 5.1) include

- administrative personnel (principals, directors, vice principals, etc.), who are responsible for maintaining the mission and vision of student learning
- teachers (veteran and newcomers), who are responsible for making sure learning is occurring in the classroom
- parents, who have a vested interest in the literacy progress of their children

Figure 5.1   Learning Community Participants

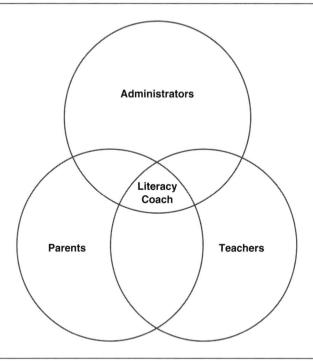

The larger, comprehensive community establishes a mission, sets goals, makes inquiries, builds knowledge, retains instruction that works, modifies instruction that doesn't work, and thinks reflectively on the progress of learning. Apart from helping individual teachers within the classroom, the literacy coach is responsible for bringing groups of school members together in productive and meaningful ways. When teachers, parents, administrations, students, and coaches come together in school learning teams, they

- strengthen their own professional knowledge
- problem solve
- celebrate successes and acknowledge challenges
- build community
- enhance instruction
- discover ways to meet individual student needs

The five school learning communities that gather for the purpose of enhancing student instruction include

- schoolwide learning communities
- teacher-coach learning communities

- teacher learning communities
- principal-coach learning communities
- parents-coach learning communities

Figure 5.2 illustrates the participants, purposes, sample activities, and suggested meeting times for each learning community.

Schoolwide Learning Communities

One by one, classes enter the auditorium. Holding hands, the kinder-gartners find a seat on the ground in front of the stage. Students in fifth grade saunter in and take their seats near the back of the room. The auditorium reverberates with the sounds of laughter, hand clap-ping, and excitement from the students.

The sound subsides when the principal emerges from behind the stage curtains and takes a seat on a rocking chair situated in front of the entire school body. Holding a book, the principal begins to read, and the entire school shares a common experience. During this Literacy Pep Rally, the school connects around a literacy event.

The *Literacy Pep Rally* is an example of a schoolwide learning com-munity event. Parents, students, teachers, administrators, staff, and coaches gather together and reaffirm their commitments to teaching and learning literacy. When the community gathers for an important schoolwide literacy event, all school personnel acknowledge the importance of literacy in their lives; they collectively connect with a common experience.

A schoolwide learning community connects all school members with a shared experience, reminds school members of their literacy mission, models the value of reading and writing in the lives of all participants, reaffirms the importance of reading and writing in students' lives, and builds motivation for students to reach school-wide literacy goals. At the beginning of the school year, it is impor-tant for the literacy coach to have a philosophical discussion with the administration concerning the school's broad vision for literacy. Incorporating input from the greater school community, the principal helps articulate a mission that establishes a shared vision (DuFour & Eaker, 1998). The entire school (principal, teachers, parents, and students) makes a commitment to change by choosing a meaningful focus (Patterson & Rolheiser, 2004). This focus is based on improved

Figure 5.2 Types of School Learning Communities

Type	Type of Meeting	Community Members	Purpose	Types of Activities	Meeting Days
Schoolwide learning community	Literacy Pep Rally	Literacy coach Teachers Principal Parents Students	❑ Connect ❑ Revisit mission ❑ Celebrate ❑ Encourage	❑ Literacy Pep Rally	Four times a year
Teacher-coach learning community	Teacher-Coach Connections	Grade-level teachers Literacy coach	❑ Set goals for the year ❑ Set goals for the month ❑ Challenges ❑ Celebrations ❑ Action plans	❑ Share information ❑ Distribute materials ❑ Coach-led professional development ❑ Discussions ❑ Goal setting ❑ Debriefing sessions ❑ Small group questions and answers	Once a month
Teacher learning community	Teacher Networks	Groups of teachers who share common literacy interests	❑ Gather information ❑ Read information about a topic ❑ Consider instructional implications ❑ Share knowledge ❑ Conduct inquiries	❑ Read professional books and articles ❑ Attend conferences ❑ Discussion groups	Once every six to eight weeks

(Continued)

Figure 5.2 (Continued)

Type	Type of Meeting	Community Members	Purpose	Types of Activities	Meeting Days
Principal-coach learning community	Principal Update Sessions	Literacy coach Principal/director	❑ Provide information ❑ Give progress reports ❑ Discuss next steps	❑ Discussion ❑ Problem/solution session	Two times a month
Parents-coach learning community	Parents-as-Partners Workshops	Literacy coach Parents Teachers	❑ Distribute information ❑ Give suggestions for literacy experiences at home ❑ Answer questions from parents ❑ Connect with community	❑ Parent Make-and-Takes ❑ Discussions	Three times a year

practice and student outcomes (Neufeld & Roper, 2003). Key questions that a literacy coach may ask include the following:

- What is your literacy vision for this school?
- In what ways do we want to help students realize their full literacy potential?
- How are we going to help students build their literacy knowledge?
- In what ways will we ask parents to assist in this mission?
- In what ways will we support teachers' efforts to provide meaningful literacy instruction?

After this discussion, the school principal, with assistance from the literacy coach, creates a Literacy Pep Rally for the beginning of the year. The Pep Rally sets the tone that reading and writing are valued processes. Activities that may be conducted at Literacy Pep Rallies include

- reading aloud a meaningful text (see Figure 5.3)
- encouraging groups of students to read their writings to the school
- celebrating schoolwide literacy successes
- challenging students to read a certain number of books throughout the year
- instituting grade-level book talks
- creating schoolwide book clubs
- explaining to parents how they can support the literacy mission at home
- inviting guest authors and illustrators to address the student population
- acknowledging individual achievements in reading and writing through a Rewards and Recognition Ceremony

In summary, the principal creates a literacy mission for the school and encourages the entire school community to work toward that mission. Literacy Pep Rallies help students, teachers, administrators, parents, and coaches revisit the school literacy mission, set goals, celebrate achievements, and connect as a literate community. Coaches and teachers work together to realize this mission when they meet in teacher-coach learning communities.

Teacher-Coach Learning Communities

At the beginning of each month, Kathy, an elementary literacy coach, gathers with a group of first grade teachers. They begin each meeting with celebrations; they share student work and anecdotes of literacy

Figure 5.3   Examples of Books for a Literacy Pep Rally

Title	Author/Illustrator	Description
Amber on the Mountain	Tony Johnston (author) Robert Duncan (illustrator)	Amber is an illiterate girl from the mountains who learns to read and write.
The Wednesday Surprise	Eve Bunting (author) Donald Carrick (illustrator)	A granddaughter teaches her grandmother how to read.
Thank You, Mr. Falker	Patricia Polacco	In this memoir, a young girl with dyslexia learns to read from her teacher, Mr. Falker.
The Day of Ahmed's Secret	Florence Parry Heide, Judith Heide Gilliland (authors) Ted Lewin (illustrator)	Ahmed, a young boy in Cairo, learns to write his name in Arabic.
Read to Me, Mama	Vishanu Rahaman (author) Lori McElrath-Eslick (illustrator)	Joseph teaches his mom how to read.
Wolf!	Becky Bloom (author) Pascal Biet (illustrator)	A hungry wolf enrolls in school and learns to read. With former foes, he travels the world reading books to children.

successes. Then they tackle their challenges. They discuss their trials and tribulations and form action plans to help them solve difficult problems. During this time, Kathy facilitates the conversation. She keeps the teachers focused on the successes and problems at hand by providing guidance and support.

VOICES FROM THE FIELD

"You have to be someone who can build trust and confidence. You gain the trust of teachers by supporting them, reassuring them, and building their confidence. You have to be so careful not to gossip about any of your teachers to their peers or the principal. As soon as you do that, you undermine any kind of trust or confidence they have in you as their coach. Gossip is so reckless in this job role."

Kathryn

The literacy coach establishes an important teacher-coach learning community when everyone gathers for a Teacher-Coach Connection session. The Teacher-Coach Connection session described earlier is an important way for literacy coaches to facilitate learning among a small group of teachers on the same grade level. During Teacher-Coach Connection sessions (see Figure 5.4), the literacy coach works with a team of teachers, once a month, for 30 minutes to one hour. This school learning group session typically occurs during a common grade-level planning period, but sometimes takes place before or after school. During this time, the coach can distribute information and materials and engage in conversations with a group of teachers about various components of literacy instruction. These connections also provide opportunities to discuss successes and challenges, work together to solve problems, analyze student work, and build team unity and rapport among groups of teachers.

Discovering Successes and Challenges and Solving Problems

The literacy coach should function from a flexible month-to-month agenda. The literacy coach sets the agenda, but the agenda should reflect the needs of the grade-level group and must incorporate suggestions from teachers. The goal of this meeting is to discover successes and challenges, brainstorm solutions to problems that are prevalent in classrooms, and focus on improvement by using documented evidence to improve practice (Hord, 1997; Neufeld & Roper, 2003). Often, the most successful Teacher-Coach Connection session involves a reiteration of successes that have occurred in individual classrooms and a systematic pursuit to solve challenges that hinder the literacy growth of students.

The successes, challenges, and action plans discussed during the Teacher-Coach Connection session can encourage teachers to focus on positives, acknowledge problems, and take steps toward resolving urgent challenges. Figure 5.5 provides an example of topics discussed during one such session. Figure 5.6 offers a "Successes, Challenges, Action Plan" template that you may wish to use in your own work with teachers.

Analyzing Student Work

Student work must guide the instructional decisions teachers make. One of the most important tasks of the literacy coach is to help teams of teachers understand the connection between student work and instructional planning. Coaching should not be driven by explaining various components of a countywide textbook adoption.

Figure 5.4   Sample Agenda of a Teacher-Coach Connection Session

AGENDA

Teacher-Coach Connection

October Session

Kindergarten

3:00–4:00 p.m.

Distribute Materials (3:00–3:05 p.m.)

- Informational texts for classroom library
- Alphabet cards
- Ink stamps and letters

Celebrations (3:05–3:10 p.m.)

- Student success
- Teaching success
- Something that worked for me last month was . . .

Challenges (3:10–3:25 p.m.)

- Student challenge
- Teacher challenge
- Something that I struggled with last month was . . .
- Action plan: How can we help you with your challenge?

Student Work Analysis (3:25–3:45 p.m.)

- Each teacher brings a sampling of a student's writing
- What does the student do well as a writer?
- What are his or her challenges?
- What are our next steps?

Goal Setting (3:45–4:00 p.m.)

- Revisit goals from last month
- Establish goals for next month

Figure 5.5   Sample Successes, Challenges, Action Plan

Successes ✳ Challenges ✳ Action Plan

These were my successes last month:

- Learned more about phonemic awareness by reading three professional articles.

- Students wrote informational texts and had command of the genre features.

- Several students moved up in their guided reading levels.

These are my current challenges:

- A student (Rob) who lacks motivation to read.

- A student (Jenny) who has difficulty brainstorming ideas for writing.

Action Plan

Challenge	Possible Solutions	Next Steps
Rob lacks motivation read.	• Match him with books that interest him. • Conduct an interest interview. • Determine what is hindering his motivation.	• Conduct survey. • Find books that match his interest. • Observe and reevaluate next week.
Jenny has difficulty brainstorming ideas for writing.	• Encourage her to bring three meaningful objects or artifacts from home to use as an impetus for writing. • Show her ways in which you use your writer's notebook.	• Discuss objects or artifacts with Jenny. • Walk through writer's notebook and notebooks of other student writers.

Coaching should be driven by observations of children as they engage in literacy practices. By observing students, recording anecdotal notes, and comparing this evidence with student work products, we attempt to answer this essential question: What do we understand about this child's reading and writing process?

At the Teacher-Coach Connection session, the coach and teachers analyze what children do as readers and writers. This is done by reviewing, dissecting, and finding themes among the corpus of observational records, anecdotal notes, and reading/writing products

Figure 5.6   Template of Successes, Challenges, Action Plan Form

Successes ✳ Challenges ✳ Action Plan

These were my successes last month:
•
•
•

These are my current challenges:
•
•

Action Plan		
Challenge	*Possible Solutions*	*Next Steps*
	•	•
	•	•

collected by the teachers and coach. These conversations support reflective teaching. When teachers study student work, they refine their teaching so that it makes sense. When groups of teachers collect student work, they allow the patterns and emerging themes to guide future instructional decisions. Some considerations when analyzing student work include the following:

- looking at the reading and writing processes of students. Ask: What are they doing as readers and writers? Why are they doing these things as readers and writers?
- helping teachers analyze what students did as readers and writers
- discussing ways that the teacher can help students grow as readers and writers after analyzing their work
- using assessment information as a basis for building content knowledge and developing instructional interventions with a group of teachers

Building Team Unity and Rapport

The teacher-coach learning community is an opportunity for the coach to bond, establish trust, and build rapport with the teachers. Teacher-coach learning teams are safe places where the coach engages in deep conversations with teachers about their celebrations, concerns, and ways forward. This is a time when the coach supports a group of teachers by bolstering their confidence, recognizing their strengths, encouraging growth, and providing an opportunity for genuine inquiry among colleagues. When teams set goals and work systematically to achieve those goals together, unity is established and a professional work environment becomes enriched. Teacher-coach learning teams are places where this important work takes place.

In summary, teachers and coaches come together as teams to discuss the literacy processes of students. By using student data (observations, reading/writing documents, assessments) to drive their discussions, the coach provides a space where teachers can make important instructional decisions. During this meeting, called *Teacher-Coach Connections*, teachers work together to solve complicated programs and celebrate successes. Their coach is present as a facilitator of this discussion. More autonomous discussions happen when teachers gather together without the coach in teacher learning communities.

VOICES FROM THE FIELD

"You have to be able to get along with a lot of very different people. I do get along with varied types of people and I know how to talk to people, so I think that's the bottom line. If you can't be diplomatic and you can't see the good in everyone and see their positives and strengths, then you're really going to struggle with coaching."

Kelly

Teacher Learning Communities

Six times during the school year, a group of teachers from various grade levels gather to study writing development. Their literacy coach has recommended various journal articles and books to broaden their understanding of writing development and instruction. The teachers have also conducted searches on their own at the local university and brought their findings to the group. The teachers take some time during their meetings to read the articles. Next, they broaden their understanding through deep conversations. They discuss what they have learned and areas where they have further interest. They connect the readings to their classroom and look for ways this new professional knowledge has influenced their instruction. Finally, they engage in action research. They study their students with enhanced knowledge of writing instruction and development. Toward the end of the year, they lead a professional development seminar to teach their colleagues about what they have learned. These Teacher Networks are important school learning communities that strengthen instruction and increase student learning.

Teacher learning communities, also called *Teacher Networks*, are school learning communities in which groups of teachers, across grade levels, develop knowledge and expertise in a literacy component of interest. Every six to eight weeks, these teacher teams gather to develop their knowledge of a specific area of literacy by reading journal articles, conducting book talks, attending conferences, and engaging in conversations with knowledgeable experts. As a culminating experience, the teachers give a brief presentation to the faculty about what they have learned regarding their topic of study (e.g., oral language, vocabulary development, reading aloud, print concepts, fluency, phonological awareness and phonics, comprehension, reading and writing in content areas, diverse learners, writing instruction, writing across the curriculum).

Learning communities provide opportunities for teachers to conduct inquiries and attempt to answer important literacy questions. Teachers can study literacy topics and gain essential content knowledge. They can then pose follow-up inquiries to explore further; disseminate knowledge across the school to broaden the content knowledge of colleagues, parents, and administration; and reflect on gained knowledge. They then modify their instructional practice based on the new knowledge gained during these important meetings.

Teacher Networks are opportunities for teachers to involve each other in "expressing their aspirations, building their awareness and developing their capabilities together" (Senge, 2000, p. 5). Teachers work independently in collaborative teams to achieve common goals of knowledge and disseminate that knowledge throughout the school community (DuFour & Eaker, 1998). Teacher Networks are led by a teacher who is nominated by the group. The literacy coach assists the lead teacher by

- helping to find appropriate journal articles and books
- connecting teachers with literacy experts
- helping teachers secure grants and funding to attend workshops and conferences
- attending book/article talks when invited

When the teacher group gathers, they can evaluate, connect, and make instructional implications by using the guides provided in Figure 5.7.

In summary, teacher learning communities are places where teachers come together to learn about literacy content areas and build their professional knowledge. This time is important because it encourages teachers to extend their learning far beyond the college courses they took to become teachers. This is a time where teachers continue their learning in a supportive group. The knowledge gained from this community can be included in the conversations that take place between principals and coaches when they meet together as a principal-coach learning community.

Principal-Coach Learning Communities

Every two weeks, Sarah, a prekindergarten literacy coach, meets with the directors of the various early learning sites. During these brief 20-minute meetings, she updates her progress as a coach. This

Figure 5.7   Template of Article/Book Study Guide

Study Guide	
Before Reading:	
What do I think I *Know*? K	What do I *Want* to know more about? W
During Reading:	
Quote From Text	Reaction, Connection, Question, Comment
After Reading:	
What have I *Learned*? L	Implications for My Classroom

is an opportunity for Sarah to discuss what she has done, what she is doing now, and what she plans to do next in the classroom. Rather than noting the weaknesses of her teachers, she highlights their strengths—acting as an advocate. When the director asks her to evaluate the performance of the teacher, she resists, reminding directors that her aim is to support her teachers and help guide them toward improved instructional practices.

Literacy coaches engage principals through *Principal Update Sessions.* Principal Update Sessions are conversations between the coach and administrators to confirm the job role of the literacy coach, report on progress in classrooms, highlight improvement in instruction and student outcomes, and reaffirm the overall literacy mission and vision. The goal of principal-coach learning communities is to engage in conversations about how administrators and teachers can support each other.

During Principal Update Sessions, the literacy coach reinforces the concept that coaching is about fostering reflective teaching and refining teaching so that meaningful, appropriate literacy instruction is implemented in the classroom. Administrators need affirmation that teachers understand the literacy objectives for their grade level and that they have the pedagogical knowledge to meet those objectives. The literacy coach is responsible for providing this narrative. Administrator update sessions provide opportunities to

- revisit the overall literacy mission and vision for the school
- provide evidence that students are reaching literacy goals and objectives
- explain your coaching role in the various classrooms
- celebrate successes and achievements made by teachers and students
- give examples of ways in which you have assisted teachers or groups of teachers
- provide ways in which the principal/director can continue to support individual teachers

Before updating administrators, it is a good idea to

- schedule twice-monthly meetings requesting no more than 20 minutes of the principal's time
- create an agenda for the meeting
- place the agenda in the participant's mailbox a day or two before the meeting
- take notes during the meeting and keep a log of your discussions

Literacy coaches must be careful not to divulge their professional opinions about individual teachers during Principal Update Sessions. These judgments should be reserved for administrators who conduct their own evaluations to determine teacher competence. In fact, when literacy coaches make evaluative comments about teachers, they undermine the trust, rapport, and confidence they worked so hard to establish throughout the year.

Some typical conversations that take place between an administrator and the literacy coach are listed below. If the administrator begins the conversation by asking for evaluative feedback, the literacy coach should redirect the conversation toward constructive statements about what has been done in the classroom and what will happen next.

Administrator	Literacy Coach
I would like you to tell me about the teacher's strengths and weaknesses.	*I understand that you would like me to give you my opinion about the teaching performance of the teacher. However, I feel that would undermine my role as a coach and advocate. Instead, I'd rather tell you about some of the things we are doing in the classroom together and how I think it is improving the reading and writing of students.*
I don't think Teacher X is doing a very good job. What is your opinion?	*I understand that you are concerned about Teacher X. However, we are working hard to overcome challenges in the classroom. These are some of the goals we are working toward this month . . .*
Overall, how would you describe the job performance of the second grade teachers?	*I really don't feel comfortable giving you generalities about the entire group. However, I can tell you what we have done this month and how I see it progressing in student work products.*

Administrators may demand evaluative input from literacy coaches, but coaches must resist, always reminding administrators they are present in classrooms to support teachers and enhance their ability as instructors. Figure 5.8 illustrates a series of steps that can guide the Principal Update Session discussion, and Figure 5.9 is a sample agenda of a Principal Update Session. Figure 5.10 offers a template that you may wish to use to guide your own discussions with school administrators.

Figure 5.8   Steps in a Principal Update Session

Steps in a Principal Update Session

Steps	Literacy Coach Role	Principal/Director Role
Step 1: Reiteration of Goals	Discuss the literacy topics that you have been addressing.	Listen to the literacy coach and ask questions.
Step 2: What Have We Done?	Discuss the ways in which you and the teachers have worked to accomplish that goal.	Ask for evidence of achievement and continue to make inquiries.
Step 3: Where are We Going?	Discuss what will happen next in classrooms.	Offer comments, ask questions, and make suggestions.
Step 4: How Can You Help?	Explain how the principal/director can continue to support current goals.	Discuss possibilities of supporting current goals.
Step 5: Comments, Questions, Suggestions	Ask the principal/director for comments, questions, and suggestions.	Provide the literacy coach with comments, questions, and suggestions.

In summary, the connections established between literacy coaches and administrators are critical. During Principal Update Sessions, the literacy coach provides evidence of how the literacy mission is being realized throughout the school. In this way, the literacy coach serves as a school ambassador, helping to create the links between the literacy mission established by the principal and the instructional practice of the teachers. The literacy coach then helps parents understand the literacy mission in parents-coach learning communities.

Parents-Coach Learning Communities

It is the end of the year and parents at an elementary school are celebrating another successful year with their children. Classes of students are prepared to sing a song they've rehearsed with the music teacher. Displays of student-created artwork hang on the walls for parents to admire. A spread of food is waiting for parents to celebrate the end of the year. Before they leave for the evening, the Parent-Teacher Association (PTA) president stands before the audience and

Figure 5.9   Sample Agenda of a Principal Update Session

AGENDA

(Sample)

Principal Update Session

9:00–9:45 a.m.

- Reiteration of Goals (9:00–9:05 a.m.)

  ○ Increase teacher's knowledge of fluency assessment.

  ○ Help teachers match students with appropriate texts.

  ○ Increase students' ability to read with speed, accuracy, and prosody.

- What Have I Done? (9:05–9:15 a.m.)

  ○ This month I am working with teachers on running records.

  ○ Teachers are learning to administer and analyze running records.

  ○ Teachers use running records to record the reading fluency of their students.

  ○ We have learned how to analyze the speed, accuracy, and prosody of students' reading.

- Where Are We Going? (9:15–9:30 a.m.)

  ○ During the next couple of weeks, I will show teachers how to match students with appropriate texts.

  ○ I will lead teachers through the following inquiry: *Why do we need to conduct running records with students? Why is it important for young readers to be fluent readers?*

  ○ Fluency will be the topic of my next Teacher-Coach Connection meeting.

  ○ Show progress using student data.

- How Can You Help? (9:30–9:40 a.m.)

  ○ Purchase video camera and videotapes so I can record how to conduct running records.

- Questions/Comments/Suggestions (9:40–9:45 a.m.)

  ○ Revisit goals from last month.

  ○ Establish goals for next month.

Figure 5.10 Principal Update Session Planning Sheet

Steps	Literacy Coach	Principal/Director Input
Step 1: *Reiteration of Goals*	Goals to review:	Principal/director input:
Step 2: *What Have We Done?*	List what you have done:	Principal/director input:
Step 3: *Where Are We Going?*	Explain where to go next:	Principal/director input:
Step 4: *How Can You Help?*	Suggest how you need help:	Principal/director input:
Step 5: *Comments, Questions, Suggestions*	Do you have any comments, questions, suggestions?	Principal/director comments:

speaks. She tells parents how they can extend literacy into their homes for the summer. When the audience leaves, they have a literacy calendar to hang on their refrigerator with reminders of simple literacy experiences in which they can engage at home.

Parents are critical partners for literacy. Thus, they deserve a prominent seat at the table reserved for building the literate lives of children. Literacy coaches can be a connective bridge to help parents bring literacy experiences into the home. At least three times a year, literacy coaches can work with the PTA to create opportunities for parents to implement rich literacy activities at home. For example, through events such as Parents-as-Partners Workshops, parents, teachers, and literacy coaches can come together to support parents in their home literacy initiatives. The purposes of parents-coach learning communities include

- sharing information with parents about extending literacy into the home
- providing suggestions to parents on how they can support their child's literacy experiences
- answering questions from parents about literacy practices that occur within the school
- offering opportunities for parents to make comments, ask questions, and offer solutions to pressing literacy problems
- eliciting input from parents on the learning of their students
- connecting parents with the school community, thus establishing strong home-school bonds

Parent-as-Partner Workshops can occur in conjunction with central events at the school. These events may include open houses, holiday celebrations, graduation ceremonies, and student performances. During these events, parents need opportunities to discuss ways to enhance literacy experiences at home, and materials can be set aside for parents to make and take to help facilitate literacy learning in the home.

Presentations to families may include the following:

- how to make reading a priority at home
- how to find appropriate books that match the students' independent and instructional reading levels
- how to encourage children to write for meaningful purposes and audiences at home

- how to encourage parents to become reading and writing examples for their children
- how to enhance literacy knowledge in children when parents are engaged in chores around town
- how to select appropriate television programs for the family to watch together
- how to find appropriate Web sites for children to navigate at home

In summary, parents are essential literacy partners. Much of what is advocated in classrooms can be easily extended into the homes of children. Literacy coaches can make a difference by creating parents-coach learning communities. Planning and preparing a parents-coach learning community, and all learning communities described in this chapter, can be a challenge for the literacy coach. The chart in Figure 5.11 can be used by the coach to plan learning communities for an entire school year.

Planning and preparation are essential for productive learning communities to run efficiently and effectively. The potential of school learning communities to enhance literacy teaching and learning is powerful. When teachers network and develop their knowledge of various content areas, their knowledge is enriched and their instructional practices change based on renewed or new understandings. When administrators meet regularly with literacy coaches, they receive updates about instructional advancements and needed support. When parents gather throughout the school year, they gain a better understanding of their role in their child's literacy learning experience. Different types of school learning communities diverge for specific purposes. They can also converge to affirm a common mission. The literacy coach is a powerful conduit in facilitating the collaborative and effective functioning of school learning communities.

Next Steps: Professional Development Suggestions

Listed below are suggested activities for coaches to use to help develop, plan, and organize various learning communities within schools.

1. With a yearly calendar, begin plotting dates and times for the various school learning teams. On your calendar, be sure to consider
   a. Literacy Pep Rallies
   b. Teacher-Coach Connections

Figure 5.11 Yearlong Planning Chart for School Learning Communities

Month	Literacy Pep Rally	Teacher-Coach Connections	Teacher Networks	Principal Update Sessions	Parents-as-Partners
September					
October					
November					
December					
January					
February					
March					
April					
May					

   c. Teacher Network Meetings

   d. Principal Update Sessions

   e. Parent-as-Partner Gatherings

2. With a group of literacy coaches, brainstorm a list of activities that can be conducted at a Literacy Pep Rally. Consider the following:

   a. How long should the Pep Rally be?

   b. What books would be appropriate for the Principal Read Aloud?

   c. How can we get children excited about reading and writing?

   d. What other schoolwide experiences can we conduct to foster engagement and motivation for reading and writing?

3. Interview a small group of teachers. Ask them the following questions about Teacher Networks:

   a. What literacy questions or topics do you believe are important to address at this time?

   b. In what areas of literacy are you most knowledgeable? How can you share this knowledge with colleagues?

4. Create an opportunity for you to engage in your own learning community with other coaches. As a group, you may want to

   a. engage in a book talk

   b. have a group meeting to discuss challenges/successes of coaching

   c. exchange coaching ideas

   d. participate in social events to boost your own energy as a coach

6

Ongoing Growth

Supporting Professional Development

In this chapter, we

- describe characteristics of high-quality professional development
- discuss strategies to support change, including school-based professional development
- present guidelines for implementing professional development initiatives

As curriculum standards and assessment mandates have changed in recent years, those responsible for overseeing reading programs, including both administrators and literacy coaches, are asked to support professional development that effectively responds to changing expectations and needs. Some factors, such as administering mandated assessments and using district-selected reading programs, are beyond the control of individual administrators, coaches, and classroom teachers. Administrators, coaches, and teachers can, however, work together on other areas such as acquiring ongoing knowledge about effective instruction and establishing a collaborative learning community. In this chapter, we provide an overview of key concepts that are part of a comprehensive literacy program's professional development activities, discuss the characteristics of high-quality professional development for teachers and coaches, and offer guidelines for supporting teacher change and implementing effective inservice programs.

VOICES FROM THE FIELD

"You have to be tactful. You have to be really honest with your coaching so that you can help teachers identify areas where they can improve as a teacher. But you have to do this in a way that builds their confidence."

Elizabeth

Comprehensive Literacy Programs

When questions arise about how best to teach early literacy and reading, most professionals identify and support five critical areas identified by the National Reading Panel (2000). In its report, the group responded to a congressional mandate to help parents, teachers, and policy makers address the key skills and areas central to effective reading instruction and achievement: phonemic awareness, phonics, fluency, vocabulary, and comprehension. The knowledge base on the components of comprehensive literacy instruction includes four elements: reading mechanics, reading comprehension, writing, and reading practice relevant to the grade level (Snow, Burns, & Griffin, 1998). Kainz and Vernon-Feagans (2007) summarized comprehensive literacy components across three grade levels, and these areas represent the content of effective professional development activities for early literacy teachers (see Table 6.1).

High-Quality Professional Development

The link between effective professional development and student achievement is clear: when schools support teachers' growth and their ability to make informed instructional decisions, student achievement improves (Darling-Hammond, 1996). All too often, traditional professional development programs require only passive involvement on

Table 6.1   Summary of Comprehensive Literacy Items at Three Grades

Grade Level	Element	Item
Kindergarten	Mechanics	• Students work on letter names. • Conventions of print are taught. • Letter recognition is taught. • Matching letters to sounds is taught. • Rhyming words and families are taught. • Students work on phonics.
	Comprehension	• Students work on new or difficult vocabulary. • Teacher reads big books and print is visible. • Teacher reads books and print is not visible.
	Writing	• Students practice writing letters of the alphabet. • Students write using inventive spelling. • Students write stories or reports.
	Practice	• Students read silently in class. • Students choose their own books to read.
First Grade	Mechanics	• Rhyming words and families are taught. • Students work on phonics. • Reading multisyllabic words is taught. • Reading fluently is taught. • Students practice reading aloud.
	Comprehension	• Students discuss new or difficult vocabulary. • Students work on vocabulary. • Teacher reads books and print is not visible. • Identifying the main idea of a story is taught. • Making predictions about text is taught.
	Writing	• Conventional spelling is taught. • Students write using inventive spelling. • Students write stories or reports. • Writing complete sentences is taught. • Composing and writing stories is taught.
	Practice	• Students read silently in class. • Students choose their own books to read.

(Continued)

Table 6.1 (Continued)

Grade Level	Element	Item
	Mechanics	• Students discuss new or difficult vocabulary. • Students read aloud.
Third grade	Comprehension	• Students talk with each other about what they read. • Students discuss different interpretations of what they read. • Students explain or support their interpretation of what they read.
	Writing	• Spelling and grammar are taught. • Writing process is taught. • Students write in journals or logs. • Students produce multiple drafts of their writing. • Students edit their work for spelling and punctuation.
	Practice	• Students read silently in class. • Students choose their own books to read.

SOURCE: Kainz, K., & Vernon-Feagans, L. (2007). The ecology of early reading development for children in poverty. *Elementary School Journal, 107,* 407–427. Publisher: University of Chicago Press.

the part of teachers. For example, teachers may listen to a presenter deliver a one-time lecture or demonstrate a new strategy. Following such a program, more often than not, teachers return to their classroom routines, applying little, if any, of the inservice information to their own instructional practices (Kent, 2004; Paez, 2003; Steyn, 2005).

Characteristics of Effective Professional Development

Richardson (2003) suggests that professional development programs are most likely to be successful when they

- involve all teachers within a single school or program area
- acknowledge and respect participants' existing beliefs and instructional practices

- seek to build consensus among participants on needed changes in the literacy program and on plans for bringing about those changes
- offer teachers a voice in both the process and the content of the experiences
- encourage collegiality
- take place over an extended period (such as several weeks, months, or even throughout the school year)
- include follow-up sessions and adjustments to the original plans
- receive ongoing building- and district-level administrative support
- receive adequate funding for materials, professional resources, and consultants

Others add that professional development is most effective when it (1) is a sustained, intensive process that focuses on appropriate content; (2) gives teachers opportunities for active, hands-on learning that is integrated into the daily life of the school; and (3) provides individual follow-up through supportive observation and feedback, staff dialogues, study groups, mentoring, and peer coaching (cf. Birman, Desimone, Porter, & Garet, 2000; Desimone, 2002; Desimone, Porter, Garet, Yoon, & Birman, 2002; Garet, Birman, Porter, Desimone, & Herman, 1999; Garet, Porter, Desimone, Birman, & Yoon, 2001; Guskey, 1994, 1999, 2003; Guskey & Sparks, 1991, 1996; Hirsh, 2005; Lieberman, 1995). Literacy coaches can support the professional development process by enabling teachers to build on their existing knowledge of teaching and learning to improve their instructional practices (Mraz, Vacca, & Vintinner, 2008).

Identifying the needs of teachers is a critical step in providing effective professional development (Guskey, 1999; Sparks & Hirsh, 1997). Figure 6.1 is an example of a survey that was distributed at the beginning of a new school year by a literacy coach to assess the professional development needs of the early literacy teachers with whom she worked. By analyzing the teachers' responses, the literacy coach was able to discern patterns in the professional development needs expressed by the group of teachers. She was also better able to understand the areas in which individual teachers believed they needed support. Using this information, the literacy coach, in collaboration with her school administrator, designed both formal and informal professional development opportunities aimed at addressing the areas in which the teachers desired support.

It is also important to design professional development in collaboration with teachers toward the goal of addressing the diverse

Figure 6.1　Sample Needs Assessment Survey

Welcome to a new school year! As we begin to make our professional development plans, we would like to know what literacy areas or topics interest you the most. For each of the items listed below, please indicate your interest in including that topic in this year's professional development activities using the following scale:

1 = I am comfortable with this topic and do not need a lot of help in this area.

2 = I would like to refresh or fine-tune my knowledge of this topic.

3 = This is a priority for me and I would like to learn a lot more about it.

Topic	Interest Level		
Phonemic awareness	1	2	3
Phonics	1	2	3
Oral language	1	2	3
Concepts of print	1	2	3
Classroom management	1	2	3
Communicating with parents	1	2	3
Organizing classroom materials	1	2	3
Assessment procedures	1	2	3
Selecting reading materials	1	2	3
Reading comprehension	1	2	3
Vocabulary development	1	2	3
Writing	1	2	3
Other (please list) _____	1	2	3

cultural characteristics that are most common for students in most schools (Farmer, Hauk, & Neumann, 2005; Kent, 2004; Schmoker, 2002). Culturally responsive teachers exhibit behaviors and use approaches that are informed by the backgrounds of their students. Culturally responsive professional development

- considers the learning styles teachers bring to workshops and presentations and folds them into resources and materials that are rich with classroom, multicultural, and multiethnic connections
- recognizes, values, and discusses the diverse ways that cultural and personal identities mediate learning styles and includes these in the content of professional workshops and presentations
- uses multidimensional assessments of learning
- empowers teachers with implicit and explicit support and development of self-regulation and socially aware critical thinking
- supports the development of cultural awareness among participants
- engages teachers in learning through a wide array of culturally authentic experiences

Characteristics of Effective
Evaluation of Professional Development

Evaluation is a critical aspect of professional development that is often overlooked (Guskey, 2002). Effective professional development evaluations collect and analyze five types of information: participants' reactions, participants' learning, organizational support and change, participants' use of new knowledge and skills, and student learning outcomes (Guskey, 2002). In Table 6.2, we present a matrix of questions, methods, and outcomes to address in evaluating these aspects of professional development.

Helping Teachers Change Beyond the
Professional Development Workshop

As teachers and coaches, we have all, at some point in our careers, attended a workshop or inservice session that was brimming with new ideas for enhancing our literacy instruction. When we left the workshop, we had every intention of using some of what we had learned with our own students. Then, when we returned to our classrooms, the day-to-day details of school life took up much of our

Table 6.2   Examples of Evaluation Information

Evaluation Level	Questions Typically Addressed	Methods and Outcomes
Participant Reactions	Did participants like the workshop? Did they believe their time was well spent? Did the information make sense? Was the presenter knowledgeable? Were room conditions comfortable?	Questionnaires administered at the end of session provide information about satisfaction.
Participant Learning	Did participants acquire new knowledge?	Pencil-and-paper assessments, simulations, and reflections provide information about knowledge and skills.
Support and Change	Was implementation publically and openly supported? Were problems addressed quickly? Were sufficient resources available? Was climate positive and productive?	District records, questionnaires, and interviews provide information about advocacy, support, accommodation, facilitation, and recognition.
Use of Knowledge	Did participants apply knowledge and skills?	Questionnaires, interviews, and observations provide information about the degree and quality of implementation.
Learning Outcomes	What was the impact on attitudes, achievement, and performance of students?	Student records, school records, questionnaires, interviews, and portfolios provide information about learning outcomes.

SOURCE: Adapted from Figure 1 in Guskey (2002).

time and energy. The workshop materials sat on our bookshelves or on our desks unused. We had hoped to put those ideas into practice, but, as time went on, it became more difficult to find the time to plan for and then to implement the changes that seemed so interesting during the workshop.

This phenomenon is a common one. Even in the best of circumstances, change can be demanding and uncomfortable. The pace at which changes are implemented depends on a number of factors. Two elements, in particular, are critical: the willingness of participants to change and their understanding of how to implement desired changes. What, then, can literacy coaches do to help teachers navigate through the change process and effectively apply the ideas they gain from inservice sessions? To support teachers as they seek to incorporate changes into their instructional routines, a number of strategies can be helpful (Kelleher, 2003; King & Newmann, 2000; Levy & Murname, 2004; Paez, 2003; Pinnell, 2006; Richardson, 2003):

- working in collaboration with individual teachers or with teams of teachers to adapt new instructional strategies to meet the needs of students
- making time for teachers to collaborate with one another—for example, establishing peer support teams, where teachers share concerns and ideas for addressing those concerns as they incorporate new strategies into their literacy programs
- encouraging teachers to visit one another's classrooms to observe the implementation of new strategies or reading programs
- encouraging peer coaching, where teachers give feedback to one another in a nonevaluative manner
- engaging in guided practice of new strategies with teachers, where the literacy coach walks the teachers through the application of new strategies
- attending conferences or workshops with teachers, and holding follow-up sessions where the content of the conference and ideas for incorporating its content are discussed
- encouraging teachers to engage in threaded discussions through e-mail as a way to support one another through the change process
- helping teachers to engage in inquiry-based teaching, where they use informal assessment tools such as their own observations of students, anecdotal notes, and work product samples to assess the effectiveness of a strategy or its impact on student learning

---

VOICES FROM THE FIELD

"Plain and simple, teachers must be readers and writers themselves if they intend to teach students about reading and writing. I just firmly believe that you cannot teach about these processes if you never engage in them yourself. So, whenever we engage in a professional development activity, I always spend some time asking teachers about what they've read and written recently. And we talk about how our own literacy practices influence our instruction."

Ben

A highly qualified teaching force is a school's most important asset, and the most important investment school boards, policy makers, administrators, and other educational leaders can make is ensuring that teachers continue to learn (American Federation of Teachers, 2002). Continuous, high-quality professional development is essential to the nation's goal of high standards of learning for every child. School administrators play an important role in making professional development a recognized priority within their school. Table 6.3 includes suggestions for some ways educational leaders can support professional development programs in their schools.

Advice for Professional Development Providers

The implementation of a professional development initiative often centers on the delivery of a formal inservice program that can serve as a catalyst for ongoing work on a particular issue or topic. To deliver an effective inservice workshop, a literacy coach needs to have appropriate content knowledge of the topic to be addressed, as well as the interpersonal skills needed to deliver the content in an engaging manner. Interpersonal behaviors associated with effective workshop leaders include the following:

- Relate to the audience in an open, honest, and approachable manner.
- Stimulate interest in the topic by relating new information to participants' background knowledge and experiences.
- Show respect for participants: Allow time for discussions that invite participants to ask questions and to work through

Table 6.3   What Can Administrators Do to Support Professional Development?

- Make time for teachers to collaborate to address student learning issues and the broader goals of the literacy program.
- Encourage the formation of study groups, such as book club lunches, where teachers discuss children's literature, or a professional materials book club, where teachers discuss literacy topics.
- Encourage peer observations, where teachers visit the classrooms of colleagues with the goal of exchanging instructional and organizational ideas.
- Allow time during regularly scheduled faculty meetings for teachers to raise questions and share observations that relate to literacy teaching and learning.
- Provide release time for teachers to attend local conferences or workshops.
- Provide funding for attending national conferences.
- Incorporate paid curriculum days into the summer calendar so that small groups of teachers can develop collaborative solutions to literacy program issues.
- Update professional resources (e.g., professional books, journals, technology resources, and videos that model lessons and strategy implementation) available to teachers through the school library.
- Establish a progress-oriented evaluation system based, in part, on teachers' self-assessments.
- Encourage teachers to participate in the development of their professional growth plans.

SOURCE: Adapted from Curry (2000), Folio (1999), Mraz et al. (2008), and Pinnell (2006).

potential challenges associated with a new idea or strategy. Answer questions patiently; avoid the use of sarcasm.
- Demonstrate enthusiasm for and interest in the topic.
- Display a sense of humor.
- Pace the workshop so that an appropriate balance between the presentation of material by the workshop leader and the active involvement of the participants is achieved.
- Read the audience: Be aware of nonverbal as well as verbal cues that indicate participants' overall responsiveness to and understanding of the topic.
- Adjust the pace, delivery, and/or content of the presentation based on participants' feedback.

Additionally, an effective professional development workshop or inservice session should engage teachers in active participation through hands-on experiences that allow them to understand the connections between theoretical information and their own instructional practices. These types of hands-on experiences can take many forms, including the following:

- role playing
- lesson demonstrations
- interviewing peers about beliefs or practices
- small-group problem solving through the use of vignettes that depict authentic classroom scenarios
- think-pair-share discussion, where each participant thinks independently about information presented and then shares his or her reflections with one other person. Following the paired sharing of ideas, a whole-group discussion can help to synthesize and extend the reflections of the participants.

No single technique or format will be effective for all inservice sessions. The literacy coach should consider the goals of the program, the background of the audience, the time of day at which the presentation is held, the length of time available for the presentation, the context, and the level of knowledge that participants bring to a particular topic. Frequent and informal evaluations by both the literacy coach and the participants can help to enhance the effectiveness of the session. For example, when delivering a workshop, the literacy coach can look for nonverbal cues from the audience indicating whether participants are eager to continue a topic or activity, or whether a topic or activity has run its course.

Informal feedback from participants is valuable as well. Rating scales or feedback forms, such as the one in Figure 6.2, can provide information on the perceived usefulness of the sessions and on concepts about which participants need more information. This feedback can help the coach to modify the sessions to meet participants' needs. At the end of each session, for example, both the coach and the teachers might exchange suggestions for future professional development. By engaging in ongoing assessment of the process and by using assessment information to adjust professional development plans, professional development programs are more likely to be more relevant to the contexts in which teachers work and, therefore, more meaningful to the participants.

Figure 6.2 Sample Feedback Form for Inservice Programs

After today's professional development program . . .

I now understand more about . . .

I would like more information on . . .

I still have questions about . . .

I have enough information on . . .

Here's what I'll do differently in my classroom . . .

Other comments . . .

Productive Professional Development for Teachers *and* Coaches

Just as teachers benefit from effective and ongoing professional development opportunities, so, too, do literacy coaches need similar opportunities to enhance their content knowledge and improve their understanding of how to respond effectively to the needs of the adult learners with whom they work. Literacy coaches benefit from both formal and informal training and support that relates to both their coaching roles and advances in the field of literacy education.

Formal training might, for example, consist of professional conference presentations, focused study groups, or inservice sessions. Informal support can be as simple as meeting consistently with other literacy coaches to collaborate on ways to address the expectations and challenges of the job. For such peer collaboration to succeed, it is essential that these initiatives receive consistent support from administrators at the building and district levels (Morgan et al., 2003; Mraz et al., 2008).

Collaboration between the school administrator and the literacy coach can be a valuable catalyst in the process of professional development program planning by working to plan ongoing, responsive professional development; helping teachers to apply gained knowledge to their literacy teaching practices; and assessing the effectiveness of professional development initiatives. When this occurs, professional development becomes more than an isolated activity; it becomes a way to consistently and collaboratively respond to literacy learning needs.

Next Steps: Professional Development Suggestions

1. Using the professional development strategy suggestions offered on page 129, survey teachers about the strategies they would most prefer to try as part of this school year's professional development program.

2. Using the summary of comprehensive literacy items provided in Table 6.1, invite grade-level teaching teams to discuss those items that they find most challenging for students to learn. Encourage them to use assessment data, including student work products, when compiling their priorities. Then, discuss professional development options that could best help them to address literacy areas of concern.

3. Administer a needs assessment survey, similar to the ones in Figure 6.1 and Figure 6.2. Working collaboratively with teachers and administrators, use the findings to plan professional development sessions for the upcoming quarter or semester.

4. Discuss with other literacy coaches the challenges of and solutions for the implementation of professional development plans.

Appendix

For Further Reading

**An Annotated Bibliography of Resources
on Literacy Instruction and Coaching**

In this appendix, we

- identify resources that provide information about important aspects of early literacy instruction, including
  - oral language development
  - concepts of print
  - phonemic awareness
  - phonics
  - fluency
  - vocabulary
  - comprehension
  - writing
  - classroom management and organization

- provide resources related to literacy coaching, including
  - books
  - articles
  - Web resources

Literacy Instruction Resources

Oral Language Development

Honig, A. S. (2007). Oral language development. *Early Child Development and Care, 177*, 581–613.

Discusses early language development and communication patterns, and presents five primary areas of focus within oral language: phonology, syntax, semantics, morphology, and pragmatics. Discusses how children attain more advanced and fine-tuned oral language.

Kies, D. A. (1993). Oral language development through storytelling: An approach to emergent literacy. *Reading Improvement, 30*, 43–48.

Discusses the value of storytelling as an instructional strategy for early language development and as a motivator for young children in the areas of reading and writing.

Kirkland, L. D., & Patterson, J. (2005). Developing oral language in primary classrooms. *Early Childhood Education Journal, 32*, 391–395.

Examines ways that teachers can both indirectly and directly teach children about language and its functions in primary classrooms through their environment, associations with literature, developmentally appropriate oral language activities, and interesting curriculum.

Riley, J., Burrell, A., & McCallum, B. (2004). Developing the spoken language skills of reception class children in two multicultural, inner-city primary schools. *British Educational Research Journal, 30*, 657–672.

Describes the results of a study of the spoken language skills of students within deprived, multicultural areas of an inner city and discusses the concept and essential importance of oral language in early literacy development. The article also describes specific strategies used to address the oral language gap of underprivileged children in an urban setting as well as their effectiveness.

Riojas-Cortez, M. (2001). It's all about talking: Oral language development in a bilingual classroom. *Dimensions of Early Childhood, 29*, 11–15.

Addresses the challenges of oral language development in a bilingual classroom setting and highlights the role of social interaction.

Woodard, C., Haskins, G., Schaefer, G., & Smolen, L. (2004). Let's talk. *Young Children, 59*, 92–95.

Describes a strategy called "Let's Talk," which is based on the idea of students using manipulatives and dialogue or "play talk" to act out scenarios from their own experiences. It includes features such as stimulating verbal information, enriching children's vocabularies, encouraging talk about activities that engage children, and practicing with the sound structure of words.

Concepts of Print

Lesiak, J. L. (1997). Research based answers to questions about emergent literacy in kindergarten. *Psychology in the Schools, 34*, 143–60.

Reviews research on emergent literacy, examines the importance of reading to children, and discusses print awareness, concepts of print, knowledge of letter names, phonemic awareness, formal reading instruction, early readers, and writing.

Share, D. L., & Gur, T. (1999). How reading begins: A study of preschoolers' print identification strategies. *Cognition and Instruction, 17*, 177–213.

Describes a study that examined noncommercial print use with four- and five-year-olds. Findings suggest that participants relied more heavily on print than on context clues.

West, L. S., & Egley, E. H. (1998). Children get more than a hamburger: Using labels and logos to enhance literacy. *Dimensions of Early Childhood, 26*, 43–46.

Describes how to incorporate the use of environmental print materials in early education through strategies such as personalized books, story walls, categorization games, and pretend play. Suggestions for reducing context clue dependence and involving families in the learning of print are provided.

Phonemic Awareness

Adams, M. J., Foorman, B. R., Lundberg, I., & Beeler, T. (1998). The elusive phoneme: Why phonemic awareness is so important and how to help children develop it. *American Educator, 22*, 18–29.

Offers suggestions for step-by-step instruction that seeks to build children's understanding of language structure. Connections between phonemic awareness development and future reading and writing are explained.

Allor, J. H., Gansle, K. A., & Denny, R. K. (2006). The stop and go phonemic awareness game: Providing modeling, practice, and feedback. *Preventing School Failure, 50*, 23–30.

Describes a study of six kindergarten students who were struggling with phonemic awareness and explains the success that they achieved using a blending and segmenting strategy called the stop and go phonemic awareness game.

Johnston, R. S., & Watson, J. E. (2004). Accelerating the development of reading, spelling and phonemic awareness skills in initial readers. *Reading and Writing: An Interdisciplinary Journal, 17*, 327–357.

A comparison of phonics instruction found that the synthetic approach was more comprehensive and effective in covering a wide range of skills than analytic approaches and, where it was used, additional instruction was not necessary.

Mraz, M., Padak, N., & Rasinski, T. (2008). *Evidence-based instruction in reading: A professional development guide to phonemic awareness.* Boston: Allyn & Bacon.

Explains key research findings about phonemic awareness and provides instructional strategies, assessment suggestions, ideas for fostering home-school connections, and suggested phonemic awareness resources.

Nichols, W. D., Rupley, W. H., Rickelman, R. J., & Algozzine, B. (2004). Examining phonemic awareness and concepts of print patterns of kindergarten students. *Reading Research and Instruction, 43,* 56–81.

Describes a study in which the authors looked at the effects of several outside factors, such as gender, socioeconomics, preschool experience, and race, in relation to the development of phonemic awareness and concepts of print development for kindergarten students.

Yopp, H. K. (1992). Developing phonemic awareness in young children. *The Reading Teacher, 45,* 696–703.

Illuminates the concept of phonemic awareness and offers tools to classroom teachers on how to enhance phonemic awareness in their students.

Zeece, P. D. (2006). Sound reading and reading sounds: The case for phonemic awareness. *Early Childhood Education Journal, 34,* 169–175.

Suggests ways in which literature can be used in the instruction of phonemic awareness; includes a list of 15 recommended children's texts.

Phonics

Cunningham, P. M. (2003). *Big words for big kids: Systematic sequential phonics & spelling.* Greensboro, NC: Carson-Dellosa.

Offers research-based strategies for implementing phonics and spelling instruction in the classroom.

Cunningham, P. M. (2005). *Phonics they use: Words for reading and writing.* Boston: Allyn & Bacon.

A practical book in which the author describes a variety of research-based instructional strategies.

Cunningham, P. M., & Hall, D. P. (2001). *Making big words: Multilevel, hands-on spelling and phonics activities.* Greensboro, NC: Frank Schaffer.

Offers an assortment of strategies for strategies for phonics and spelling instruction.

Mather, N., Sammons, J., & Schwartz, J. (2006). Adaptations of the names test: Easy-to-use phonics assessments. *The Reading Teacher, 60,* 114–122.

Examines the effects of using an adapted version of Cunningham's Names Test as a phonics assessment. Adaptations include reordering the first and last names by difficulty level and creating a downward extension of the Names Test that would be more appropriate for use with first- and second-grade students, as well as with struggling readers.

Pinnell, G. S., & Fountas, I. C. (1998). *Word matters*. Portsmouth, NH: Heinemann.

Offers both theoretical and practical elements of word study, including strategies that focus on phoneme-grapheme relationships, word patterns, and spelling.

Zimmerman, B., Padak, N., & Rasinski, T. (2008). *Evidence-based instruction in reading: A professional development guide to phonics*. Boston: Allyn & Bacon.

Explains key research findings about phonics and provides instructional strategies, assessment suggestions, ideas for fostering home-school connections, and suggested phonics resources.

Fluency

Hasbrouck, J. E., Ihnot, C., & Rogers, G. H. (1999). "Read Naturally": A strategy to increase oral reading fluency. *Reading Research and Instruction, 39*, 27–18.

Explains how to implement an instructional strategy for increasing fluency.

Kuhn, M. (2004). Helping students become accurate, expressive readers: Fluency instruction for small groups. *The Reading Teacher, 58*, 338–344.

Provides strategy suggestions for effective fluency instruction.

Padak, N., & Rasinski, T. (2008). *Evidence-based instruction in reading: A professional development guide to fluency*. Boston: Allyn & Bacon.

Explains key research findings about fluency and provides instructional strategies, assessment suggestions, ideas for fostering home-school connections, and suggested fluency resources.

Schwanenflugel, P. J., Meisinger, E. B., Wisenbaker, J. M., Kuhn, M. R., Strauss, G. P., & Morris, R. D. (2006). Becoming a fluent and automatic reader in the early elementary school years. *Reading Research Quarterly, 41*, 496–522.

In addition to developing a research-based model for fluency instruction, this study evaluated the impact that fluency had on reading comprehension. The work has value for continuing efforts to establish the importance of fluency to early literacy.

Vocabulary

Baker, S., Simmons, D., & Kame'enui, E. J. (1998). Vocabulary acquisition: Research bases. In D. C. Simmons & E. J. Kame'enui (Eds.), *What reading research tells us about children with diverse learning needs: Bases and basics* (pp. 183–218). Mahwah, NJ: Erlbaum.

The authors address the research on vocabulary, as well as its instruction and implementation.

Bear, D., Invernizzi, M., Templeton, S., & Johnson, F. (2000). *Words their way: Word study for phonics, vocabulary, and spelling instruction* (2nd ed.). Upper Saddle River, NJ: Prentice Hall.

This book coordinates student learning with the appropriate developmental levels. It contains ready-to-use word study, spelling, vocabulary, and phonics activities.

Bear, D. R., & Templeton, S. (1998). Explorations in developmental spelling: Foundations for learning and teaching phonics, spelling, and vocabulary. *The Reading Teacher, 52*(3), 222–242.

Explains categorizations and stages of development within phonics, spelling, and vocabulary knowledge.

Elley, W. B. (1989). Vocabulary acquisition from listening to stories. *Reading Research Quarterly, 14*, 174–187.

A study in which the researchers found that listening to stories read aloud had a significant effect on vocabulary acquisition, even when new vocabulary was not explicitly defined.

Newton, E., Padak, N., & Rasinski, T. (2008). *Evidence-based instruction in reading: A professional development guide to vocabulary.* Boston: Allyn & Bacon.

Explains key research findings about vocabulary and provides instructional strategies, assessment suggestions, ideas for fostering home-school connections, and suggested vocabulary resources.

Comprehension

Boulware-Gooden, R., Carreker, S., Thornhill, A., & Joshi, R. M. (2007). Instruction of metacognitive strategies enhances reading comprehension and vocabulary achievement of third-grade students. *The Reading Teacher, 61*, 70–77.

This article discusses instructional practices that best promote comprehension and vocabulary development.

Guthrie, J. T., Hoa, A. L. W., Wigfield, A., Tonks, S. M., Humenick, N. M., & Littles, E. (2007). Reading motivation and reading comprehension growth in the later elementary years. *Contemporary Educational Psychology, 32*, 282–313.

This study focuses on the connection between reading motivation and reading comprehension.

Marcell, B. (2007). Traffic light reading: Fostering the independent usage of comprehension strategies with informational text. *The Reading Teacher, 60*, 778–781.

Focuses on creating students who are thoughtful and engaged readers and uses stop and go questions to encourage students to independently monitor and revise their comprehension.

Parker, M., & Hurry, J. (2007). Teachers' use of questioning and modeling comprehension skills in primary classrooms. *Educational Review, 59*, 299–314.

This study explores the extent to which comprehension strategies are explicitly taught within the literacy hour—something the authors consider a necessity—and opportunities that are provided for children to generate their own questions.

Rasinski, T., & Padak, N. (2008). *Evidence-based instruction in reading: A professional development guide to comprehension*. Boston: Allyn & Bacon.

Explains key research findings about comprehension and provides instructional strategies, assessment suggestions, ideas for fostering home-school connections, and suggested comprehension resources.

Reis, S. M., McCoach, D. B., Coyne, M., Schreiber, F. J., Eckert, R. D., & Gubbins, E. J. (2007). Using planned enrichment strategies with direct instruction to improve reading fluency, comprehension, and attitude toward reading: An evidence-based study. *Elementary School Journal, 108*, 3–24.

This study investigated the effects of an enriched reading program on reading comprehension, oral reading fluency, and attitude toward reading in two elementary schools. The researchers exposed students to books within their areas of interest and to daily supported independent reading of challenging self-selected books using differentiated reading instruction.

Smith, L. A. (2006). Think-aloud mysteries: Using structured, sentence-by-sentence text passages to teach comprehension strategies. *The Reading Teacher, 59*, 764–773.

The strategy described in this article uses a continuum of sentences from general to increasingly specific to describe a mystery topic. One important component to this strategy is the think-aloud element that allows the student to focus on comprehension.

Writing

Calkins, L. (1994). *The art of teaching writing*. Portsmouth, NH: Heinemann.

In this seminal text, Calkins provides the philosophical framework for why it is so important that our young children write.

Fletcher, R., & Portalupi, J. (2001). *Writing workshop*. Portsmouth, NH: Heinemann.

This practical book helps teachers understand how to develop a writing workshop in their classrooms. The authors offer advice on how to create time and space for writing in the classroom, confer with writers, and evaluate writing.

Graves, D. (2004). What I've learned from teachers of writing. *Language Arts, 82*(2), 88–94.

In his illuminating article, Graves, one of the most important researchers in writing instruction, describes what he has learned from writing teachers.

Hansen, J. (2001). *When writers read*. Portsmouth, NH: Heinemann.

In her book, Hansen makes powerful connections between reading and writing. Five concepts underscore the importance of an effective reading-writing program: voice, decisions, time, response, and self-discipline.

Ray, K., & Cleveland, L. (2004). *About the authors: Writing workshop with our youngest writers*. Portsmouth, NH: Heinemann.

This book, geared toward writers in the early grades, provides advice for teachers as they implement writing instruction in their classrooms. Using multiple examples of student work, the authors show how teachers can teach writing in developmentally appropriate ways.

Classroom Management and Organization

Bondy, E., Ross, D. D., Gallingane, C., & Hambacher, E. (2007). Creating environments of success and resilience: Culturally responsive classroom management and more. *Urban Education, 42*, 326–348.

Describes the effective classroom management practices of two teachers in an urban setting. The article addresses the distinct challenges that setting presents, and explains the methods two teachers used to overcome those challenges.

Rowan, L. O. (2007). Making classrooms bully-free zones: Practical suggestions for educators. *Kappa Delta Pi Record, 43*, 182–183, 185.

Discusses the need for better teacher preparation programs, new teacher induction, and professional development initiatives that place greater emphasis on acquiring and practicing effective classroom management strategies.

Coaching Resources

Books

Allen, J., Szymusiak, K., & Sibberson, F. (2006). *Becoming a literacy leader: Supporting learning and change*. Portland, ME: Stenhouse.

Highlights the work of an elementary school teacher who became a literacy specialist. Includes advice on organizing a literacy room, coaching new and veteran teachers, and funding staff development.

Bean, R. M. (2004). *The reading specialist: Leadership for the classroom, school, and community: Solving problems in teaching literacy*. New York: Guilford Press.

Focuses on the history, roles, responsibilities, challenges, and the need for reading specialists.

Casey, K. (2006). *Literacy coaching: The essentials*. Portsmouth, NH: Heinemann.

Explains the roles and responsibilities of literacy coaches; includes real-life examples of what coaches need to know, as well as information on how to use data to inform instruction.

Dozier, C. (2006). *Responsive literacy coaching: Tools for creating and sustaining purposeful change*. Portland, ME: Stenhouse.

Discusses being a responsive literacy coach, highlights frequently asked questions about coaching and assessment, and discusses how to broaden the role of the literacy coach.

Moxley, D. E., & Taylor, R. T. (2006). *Literacy coaching: A handbook for school leaders*. Thousand Oaks, CA: Corwin Press.

Serves as a resource for school leaders as they implement literacy coaching programs; offers advice on creating a collaborative learning community for literacy.

Puig, E. A., & Froelich, K. S. (2006). *The literacy coach: Guiding in the right direction*. Boston: Allyn & Bacon.

This resource for reading specialists and literacy coaches includes both theoretical and practical information about their roles and responsibilities. It helps prepare coaches and specialists to implement literacy programs at school and district levels.

Rodgers, A., & Rodgers, E. (2007). *The effective literacy coach: Using inquiry to support teaching and learning*. New York: Teachers College Press.

Examines the importance of literacy coaching in improving instructional practice. Highlights the importance of teacher reflection and collaborative inquiry.

Toll, C. A. (2006). *Literacy coach's desk reference: The processes and perspectives for effective coaching*. Urbana, IL: The National Council of Teachers of English.

This book gives practical strategies for dealing with daily concerns such as conferencing with individual teachers, facilitating group meetings, providing demonstration lessons, providing services to the entire school, and providing services to students.

Walpole, S., & McKenna, M. C. (2004). *The literacy coach's handbook: A guide to research-based practice*. New York: Guilford Press.

Explains what a literacy coach does and how to become one. Helps coaches define their roles and responsibilities and provides guidance on how to accomplish their goals.

Articles

Blachowicz, C., Obrochta, C., & Fogelberg, E. (2005). Literacy coaching for change. *Educational Leadership, 62*, 55–58.

Looks at literacy coaching in the Evanston/Skokie School District and argues that a coach's major role is to provide professional development and support for teachers to improve classroom instruction.

Cobb, C. (2005). Speaking to administrators and reading specialists literacy teams: Sharing leadership to improve student learning. *The Reading Teacher, 58*, 472–474.

Explains the rationale behind a team approach to literacy leadership and provides practical suggestions for establishing effective collaboration between literacy coaches and school administrators.

Deussen, T., Coskie, T., & Robinson, L. (2007). *"Coach" can mean many things: Five categories of literacy coaches and Reading First issues and answers* (Report No. 007). Washington, DC: National Center for Education Evaluation and Regional Assistance. (ERIC Document Reproduction Service No. ED497517)

This study addresses the background, skills, and qualifications of Reading First literacy coaches, as well as how they spend their time and define the focus of their work.

Johnson, M. (2006). Preparing reading specialists to become competent travelers in urban settings. *Urban Education, 41,* 402–426.

A qualitative study that looks at teacher education methods and teacher preparation and explores the issue of focusing on process rather than on outcomes.

Symonds, K. W. (2003). *Literacy coaching: How school districts can support a long-term strategy in a short-term world.* San Francisco: San Francisco Bay Area School Reform Collaborative.

Describes how three San Francisco Bay Area school districts used literacy coaching to organize, fund, and support literacy instruction.

Useful Web Sites

http://www.busyteacherscafe.com/literacy_coaches.htm

A resource page for literacy coaches with opportunities to share and provide support for each other. Includes ideas for units, literacy centers, and classroom management.

http://www.busyteacherscafe.com

Includes suggestions for fluency instruction and assessment, as well as a list of Web sites related to fluency topics.

http://www.choiceliteracy.com

For K–12 literacy leaders. Provides tools, guides, literacy lessons and advice, articles, professional-quality videos, professional development programs, and sample observation forms. *Subscription required.*

http://drwilliampmartin.tripod.com/classm.html

A collection of classroom management and discipline Web sites and articles. There are tips for various grade levels, teacher experience levels, and student ability levels. Organizational and preventive strategies are also included.

http://www.learnnc.org/

Contains an assortment of resources from lesson plans to hot topics for specific grade levels. Articles and professional literature are provided for a variety of issues, including classroom management, diverse learners, and professional skills development.

http://www.literacycoachingonline.org
Literacy Coaching Clearinghouse. Provides access to research and best practices to enhance the knowledge base of literacy coaches. A joint venture of IRA and NCTE.

http://www.literacycoachingresources.info/ResourcesonCoachin.html
Includes coaching Web sites, the Literacy Coaching Clearinghouse articles, and IRA and NCTE Standards documents.

http://www.members.tripod.com/comptoolbelt
Created by reading specialists in the Portsmouth School District, this is a site for literacy coach resources such as videos, Listservs, units of study, NCTE Standards for Coaching, and IRA Literacy Coaching.

http://www.ncte.org/collections/literacycoach
A collection of online resources for literacy coaches to deepen their literacy understandings, instructional methods, and assessment strategies.

http://www.nea.org/classmanagement/archive.html
Articles organized by specific problems that may arise, such as time conflicts, disruptive behavior, or group work.

http://www.reachoutandread.org
Reach Out and Read is a national nonprofit organization that promotes early literacy by giving new books to children and advice to parents about the importance of reading aloud.

http://www.readingonline.org
Web site of the IRA. Offers numerous resources for literacy coaches, teachers, and administrators.

http://reading.uoregon.edu
Focuses on phonemic awareness, alphabetic principles, fluency with text, vocabulary, and comprehension. Includes definitions and descriptions of the research and theories, describes how to assess them, and provides instructional examples.

http://www.readwritethink.org
In partnership with the International Reading Association (IRA) and National Council of Teachers of English (NCTE), this site offers

resources broken down by topic and grade level. It is a practical store-house containing lesson plans, student materials, and Web resources.

http://www.specialconnections.ku.edu/cgi-bin/cgiwrap/spec
conn/index.php

Focuses on staff development or literacy coaching specifically related to students with special needs.

http://www.wordplays.com/p/index

A word study site that has various resources for word challenges and playing with words using anagrams.

Next Steps: Professional Development Suggestions

1. Select a resource from those provided in this appendix. Use that resource as the basis for a book club or study group with a small group of teachers or a group of literacy coaches.

2. As a new literacy coach, interview an experienced literacy coach about his or her coaching experiences and advice for new coaches.

3. Explore professional resources, such as books, articles, and Web-based materials to extend the list of resources provided here.

References

Algozzine, B., & Ysseldyke, J. E. (2006). *Effective instruction for students with special needs*. Thousand Oaks, CA: Corwin Press.

Allington, R. L., & Walmsley, S. A. (2007). *No quick fix: Rethinking literacy programs in America's elementary schools*. New York: Teachers College Press.

American Federation of Teachers. (2002). *Principles for professional development: AFT's guidelines for creating professional development programs that make a difference*. Washington, DC: Author.

Au, K. H. (2002). Elementary programs: Guiding change in a time of standards. In S. B. Wepner, D. S. Strickland, & J. T. Feeley (Eds.), *The administration and supervision of reading programs* (pp. 42–58). New York: Teachers College Press.

Basketball-plays-and-tips.com. Basketball coach quotes: Phil Jackson quotes. Retrieved from http://www.basketball-plays-and-tips.com/phil-jackson-quotes.html.

Bean, R. M. (2004). Promoting effective literacy instruction: The challenge for literacy coaches. *The California Reader*, 37(3), 58–63.

Bean, R. M., & DeFord, D. (2007). *Do's and don'ts for literacy coaches: Advice from the field*. Retrieved November 1, 2007, from the Literacy Coaching Clearinghouse Web site: http://www.literacycoachingonline.org

Bean, R. M., Trovato, C. A., & Hamilton, R. (1995). Focus on Chapter 1 reading programs: Views of reading specialists, classroom teachers, and principals. *Reading Research and Instruction*, 34, 204–221.

Beaver, J. (1999). *Developmental reading assessment*. Upper Saddle River, NJ: Pearson-Scott Foresman.

Birman, B. F., Desimone, L., Porter, A. C., & Garet, M. S. (2000). Designing professional development that works. *Educational Leadership*, 57(8), 28–33.

Blachowicz, C., Obrochta, C., & Fogelberg, E. (2005). Literacy coaching for change. *Educational Leadership*, 62(6), 55–58.

Brainyquote.com. Vince Lombardi quotes. Retrieved from http://www.brainyquote.com/quotes/authors/v/vince_lombardi.html.

Byrne, B., & Fielding-Barnsley, R. (1991). Evaluation of a program to teach phonemic awareness to young children. *Journal of Educational Psychology*, 83(4), 451–455.

Curry, S. (2000). Portfolio-based teacher assessment. *Thrust for Educational Leadership*, 29(3), 34–37.

Darling-Hammond, L. (1996). What matters most: A competent teacher for every child. *Phi Delta Kappan*, 78, 193–200.

Desimone, L. (2002). How can comprehensive school reform models be successfully implemented? *Review of Educational Research, 72*(3), 433–479.

Desimone, L., Porter, A. C., Garet, M. S., Yoon, K., & Birman, B. F. (2002). Effects of professional development on teachers' instruction: Results from a three year longitudinal study. *Educational Evaluation and Policy Analysis, 24*(2), 81–112.

Dole, J. A. (2004). The changing role of the reading specialist in school reform. *The Reading Teacher, 57*, 462–471.

Dole, J. A., & Donaldson, R. (2006). "What am I supposed to do all day?" Three big ideas for the reading coach. *The Reading Teacher, 59*(5), 486–488.

DuFour, R. (2003). Building a professional learning community. *School Administrator, 60*(5), 13–18.

DuFour, R., & Eaker, R. (1998). *Professional learning communities at work: Best practices for enhancing student achievement.* Reston, VA: Association for Supervision and Curriculum Development.

Dunn, L. M., & Dunn, L. (1981). *Peabody Picture Vocabulary Test: Revised manual for Form L and M.* Circle Pines, MN: American Guidance Service.

Farmer, J., Hauk, S., & Neumann, A. M. (2005). Negotiating reform: Implementing process standards in culturally responsive professional development. *The High School Journal, 88*(4), 59–71.

Farr, R. (1992). Putting it all together: Solving the reading assessment puzzle. *The Reading Teacher, 46*(1), 26–37.

Folio, E. (1999). What are teachers talking about? Peer conversations as professional dialogue. *ERS Spectrum, 17*(1), 16–22.

Fox, D. (2004, November–December). Making the most of reading assessments: Principals play a key role in helping their schools develop the tools, support and structure needed to use unit tests to improve instructional practice. *Leadership.* Retrieved December 14, 2007, from http://findarticles.com/p/articles/mi_m0HUL/is_2_34/ai_n8967453

Garet, M., Birman, B., Porter, A., Desimone, L., & Herman, R. (1999). *Designing effective professional development: Lessons from the Eisenhower program.* Washington, DC: U.S. Department of Education.

Garet, M., Porter, A., Desimone, L., Birman, B., & Yoon, K. (2001). What makes professional development effective? Results from a national sample of teachers. *American Educational Research Journal, 38*(4), 915–945.

Guskey, T. R. (1994, April). *Professional development in education: In search of the optimal mix.* Paper presented at the Annual Meeting of the American Educational Research Association, New Orleans, LA.

Guskey, T. R. (1999). *Evaluating professional development.* Thousand Oaks, CA: Corwin Press.

Guskey, T. R. (2002). Does it make a difference? Evaluating professional development. *Educational Leadership, 59*(6), 45–51.

Guskey, T. R. (2003). What makes professional development effective? *Phi Delta Kappan, 84*, 748–750.

Guskey, T. R., & Sparks, D. (1991). What to consider when evaluating professional development. *Educational Leadership, 49*(3), 73–76.

Guskey, T. R., & Sparks, D. (1996). Exploring the relationship between professional development and improvements in student learning. *Journal of Professional Development, 17*(4), 34–38.

Hall, B. (2004). Literacy coaches: An evolving role. *Carnegie Reporter, 3*(1). Retrieved on September 27, 2007, from http://www.carnegie.org/reporter/09/literacy/index.html

Hindson, B., Byrne, B., Fielding-Barnsley, R., Newman, C., Hine, D., & Shankweiler, D. (2005). Assessment and early instruction of preschool children at risk for reading disability. *Journal of Educational Psychology, 97*, 687–704.

Hirsh, S. (2005). Professional development and closing the achievement gap. *Theory into Practice, 44*, 38–44.

Hord, S. (1997). *Professional learning communities: Communities of continuous inquiry and improvement.* Austin, TX: Southwest Educational Development Laboratory.

International Reading Association. (2004). *The role and qualifications of the reading coach in the United States.* A position statement of the International Reading Association. Newark, DE: Author.

International Reading Association. (2006). IRA surveys coaches. *Reading Today, 23*(5), 1–3.

International Reading Association. (2007). *Teaching reading well: A synthesis of the International Reading Association's research on teacher preparation for reading instruction.* Newark, DE: Author.

Jonston, D., & Lawrence, J. (2004, November–December). Using data to inform instruction: While test scores are accepted as a measure of school effectiveness, the data should also be used in a more student-centric way to inform targeted instruction. *Leadership.* Retrieved December 14, 2007, from http://findarticles.com/p/articles/mi_m0HUL/is_2_34/ai_n8967452

Kainz, K., & Vernon-Feagans, L. (2007). The ecology of early reading development for children in poverty. *Elementary School Journal, 107*, 407–427.

Kelleher, J. (2003). A model for assessment-driven professional development. *Phi Delta Kappan, 84*, 751–756.

Kent, A. M. (2004). Improving teacher quality through professional development. *Education, 124*, 427–535.

King, M. B., & Newmann, F. M. (2000). Will teacher learning advance school goals? *Phi Delta Kappan, 81*, 576–580.

Kohn, A. (1999). *The schools our children deserve: Moving beyond traditional classrooms and tougher standards.* New York: Houghton Mifflin.

Lapp, D., Fisher, D., Flood, J., & Frey, N. (2003). Dual role of the urban reading specialist. *Journal of Staff Development, 24*(2), 33–36.

Lashway, L. (1997). *Leading with vision.* Eugene, OR: ERIC Clearinghouse on Educational Management.

Levy, F., & Murname, R. J. (2004). A role for technology in professional development? Lessons from IBM. *Phi Delta Kappan, 85*, 728–734.

Lieberman, A. (1995). Practices that support teacher development. *Phi Delta Kappan, 76*, 591–596.

Louis, K. S., & Kruse, S. D. (1995). *Professionalism and community: Perspectives on reforming urban schools.* Thousand Oaks, CA: Corwin Press.

Maheady, L., Mallette, B., & Harper, G. F. (1996). The pair tutoring program: An early field-based experience to prepare preservice general educators to work with students with special learning needs. *Teacher Education and Special Education, 19*(4), 277–297.

Mallette, B., Maheady, L., & Harper, G. F. (1999). The effects of reciprocal peer coaching on preservice general educators' instruction of students with special learning needs. *Teacher Education and Special Education, 22*(4), 201–216.

Mallette, M. H., Kile, R. S., Smith, M. M., McKinney, M., & Readence, J. E. (2000). Constructing meaning about literacy difficulties: Preservice teachers beginning to think about pedagogy. *Teaching and Teacher Education, 16*(5–6), 593–612.

Marzano, R. J. (2003). *What works in schools: Translating research into action.* Alexandria, VA: Association for Supervision and Curriculum Development.

Medina, A. L. (2008). *Do a triple take: Using a tri-perspective form for teacher observation.* Manuscript in preparation.

Morgan, D. N., Saylor-Crowder, K., Stephens, D., Donnelly, A., DeFord, D. E., & Hamel, E. (2003). Managing the complexities of a statewide reading initiative. *Phi Delta Kappan, 85,* 139–145.

Morrow, L. M. (2005). *Literacy development in the early years: Helping children read and write.* Boston: Allyn & Bacon.

Moxley, D., & Taylor, R. T. (2006). *Literacy coaching: A handbook for school leaders.* Thousand Oaks, CA: Corwin Press.

Mraz, M., & Kissel, B. (2007). *Focus on: Teaching and testing in early reading.* Alexandria, VA: Educational Research Service.

Mraz, M., Vacca, J. V., & Vintinner, J. (2008). Professional development. In S. Wepner & D. Strickland (Eds.), *The administration and supervision of reading programs* (4th ed., pp. 133–143). New York: Teachers College Press.

National Reading Panel. (2000). *Teaching children to read: An evidence-based assessment of the scientific research literature on reading and its implications for reading instruction* (NIH Publication No. 00-4769). Washington, DC: National Institute of Child Health and Human Development. Retrieved August 22, 2007, from http://www.nichd.nih.gov/publications/nrp/upload/small book_pdf.pdf

Neufeld, B., & Roper, D. (2003). *Coaching: A strategy for developing instructional capacity.* Washington, DC: The Aspen Institute Program on Education.

Neuman, S., Copple, C., & Bredekamp, S. (2001). Teacher handout: Assessing young children's literacy development. In *Learning to Read and Write: Developmentally Appropriate Practices for Young Children.* Washington, DC: National Association for the Education of Young Children.

No Child Left Behind Act of 2001, 20 U.S.C. §§ 6301 et seq. (2002). Retrieved December 22, 2007, from http://www.ed.gov/policy/elsec/leg/esea02/107-110.pdf

Paez, M. (2003). Gimme that school where everything's scripted! One teacher's journey toward effective literacy instruction. *Phi Delta Kappan, 84,* 757–763.

Patterson, D., & Rolheiser, C. (2004). *Creating a culture of change.* Oxford, OH: National Staff Development Council.

Pinnell, G. S. (2006). Every child a reader: What one teacher can do. *The Reading Teacher, 60*(1), 78–83.

Pipes, G. (2004). *What are they really doing? A mixed methodology inquiry into the multi-faceted role of the elementary reading specialist.* Unpublished doctoral dissertation, University of Alabama, Tuscaloosa.

Richardson, V. (2003). The dilemmas of professional development. *Phi Delta Kappan, 84,* 401–406.

Schmoker, M. (2002). Up and away. *Journal of the National Staff Development Council, 23*(4), 10–13.

Senge, P. (2000). *Schools that learn: A fifth discipline for parents, educators, and everyone who cares about education.* New York: Doubleday.

Shanklin, N. (2006). *What are the characteristics of effective literacy coaching?* Retrieved November 1, 2007, from http://www.literacycoachingonline.org

Shaw, M. L., Smith, W. E., Chesler, B. J., & Romeo, L. (2005). Moving forward: The reading specialist as literacy coach. *Reading Today, 22*(6), 6.

Snow, C. E., Burns, S. M., & Griffin, P. (Eds.). (1998). *Preventing reading difficulties in young children.* Washington, DC: National Academy Press.

Sparks, D., & Hirsh, S. (1997). *A new vision for staff development.* Alexandria, VA: Association for Supervision and Curriculum Development.

Steyn, G. M. (2005). Exploring factors that influence the effective implementation of professional development programmes on invitational education. *Journal of Invitational Theory and Practice, 11,* 7–34.

Strickland, D. S. (2002). Pre-elementary reading programs: New expectations. In S. B. Wepner, D. S. Strickland, & J. T. Feeley (Eds.), *The administration and supervision of reading programs* (3rd ed., pp. 29–41). New York: Teachers College Press.

Tatum, A. W. (2004). A road map for reading specialists entering schools without exemplary reading programs: Seven quick lessons. *The Reading Teacher, 58*(1), 28–39.

Toll, C. (2005). *The literacy coach's survival guide: Essential questions and practical answers.* Newark, DE: International Reading Association.

U.S. Department of Education. (2002). *The No Child Left Behind Act of 2001.* Retrieved January 11, 2002, from http://www.ed.gov/offices/OESE/esea/NCLBexecsumm.pdf

Walker, B. (2008). *Diagnostic teaching of reading.* Upper Saddle River, NJ: Pearson Prentice Hall.

Index

CORWIN PRESS

The Corwin Press logo—a raven striding across an open book—represents the union of courage and learning. Corwin Press is committed to improving education for all learners by publishing books and other professional development resources for those serving the field of PreK–12 education. By providing practical, hands-on materials, Corwin Press continues to carry out the promise of its motto: **"Helping Educators Do Their Work Better."**

The mission of the International Reading Association is to promote reading by continuously advancing the quality of literacy instruction and research worldwide.